AMERICAN WOMAN

AMERICAN•WOMAN

R E V I S I T E D

HELLO
I am

still
^ Lost and Found
in Oklahoma

Pam Fleischaker

FULL CIRCLE PRESS : OKLAHOMA CITY

First edition, first printing 2001
Revisited edition, first printing 2007

Printed and bound in the United States of America

Book, text, and jacket designed by Carl Brune
Edited by Shauna Lawyer Struby and Mike Easterling
Published by Full Circle Press, a division of Full Circle Bookstore,
50 Penn Place, Oklahoma City, OK 73118

ISBN 978-0-9661460-4-2

For David, Joey and Emily
sunshine when skies are gray
and
in memory of Dottie Mandell

CONTENTS

very venture brings discoveries, and in this revised edition, I discovered gratitude anew.

Thanks to Debora Morey for her support and good nature; Shauna Lawyer Struby and Carl Brune, again, for their talent, endurance and willingness to bond, as Shauna says, via computer. Thanks, also, to Susan Moore at Full Circle Bookstore who said, simply, "More of the same."

Thanks, to my sister, Missy, for the caret, and my dad, Bud, for his continued wisdom; to David, my favorite computer geek, for his love, perseverance and insights; and to Joey for his gentle patience, photography and lesson in working the count.

Thanks to Emily, in particular, for adding this to her growing to-do list. Her voice, her attitude and her perfect pitch are a pleasure.

Thanks again, and never too often, to Mike Easterling who I hope will remain my editor for life. He lives in New Mexico now, and working with him over green-chili stew almost beats the newsroom.

In the summer of 2004 my good friend and colleague Toby Thompson died. I miss his wicked humor and his fine taste, and I could have used his help on this project. I could kill him for dying. But I imagine he's reading this somewhere, sipping wine and laughing all the way.

I am especially grateful, still, to Jim Tolbert. His resolve and determination got me there. It continues to be a privilege.

ACKNOWLEDGMENTS

n compiling this book, I have had a wonderful cheering section of friends and family, many of whom were early readers of the drafts. Thanks to Anne Barnstone, J.B. Bleckley, Ellen Feuerborn, Joie Singer, Deborah Lynch, Mimi Mager and Marcy Roberts for the thumbs-up to keep moving.

Susan Estrich read and re-read, gave me valuable insights and told me, as she always does, to go for it. My buddies Phil Bacharach and Toby Thompson are both terrific writers who also read early drafts and put up with my constant requests for advice. Mary Corson wins the prize for the most ideas on the back of an envelope and Jon Sackler wins the sickest title entry award. Janet Wilson is always there for me no matter how badly I behave, with tough talk and a great meal, and Tom Wilson helps me see things more clearly.

Kevin Sullivan has been putting words into other people's mouths for years, and we all sound better for it. I thank him, as ever, for his help.

Bill Bleakley, owner and publisher of the Oklahoma Gazette, has provided me and others at the paper with the freedom and the forum to write what I believe, and I am grateful to him for his support.

Mike Easterling, editor of the Oklahoma Gazette and my good friend for more than a decade, taught me to be a journalist. He taught me to put my thoughts into honest, and fewer, words; to make my opinions count for something; to write from my heart and never be a wimp in the face of authority. Never.

Jim Tolbert, the brains behind Full Circle Bookstore and Full Circle Press, is a man of great class and integrity. I can't imagine a finer publisher and guide. Shauna Struby has been a gentle but prodding editor, who helped me get over my unnatural attachment to parentheses. Carl Brune is a talented artist and designer, always open to my ideas and vision.

Debbie Fleischaker has worked overtime on me for 30 years. Her intellectual input is important, but mostly it's the jewelry. I'd be unadorned without her.

Missy Mandell lost all her eye make-up reading an early version of this book on an airplane. Her comments and suggestions were, without exception, on target. Her editing notes go in my keepsake box forever. But mostly, her pride and enthusiasm in my accomplishments are a great gift. But I'm not surprised. There really never were such devoted sisters.

I learned everything I needed to know from Bud and Dottie Mandell. They put the music in my life.

And David Fleischaker, my best friend, has read everything I've written 'til his hair has fallen out. When I get cold feet, he warms them. He can always be counted on for the smartest, sharpest and most honest feedback. Even when he's wrong.

FOREWORD 2007
Emily Fleischaker

have a confession to make. I never read your book, Mom. This book, originally published in 2001, the year I graduated from high school. I have my own copy, with a note from you: "For my wonderful American girl, soon to be a woman! Love, Mom."

I gave copies of your book to my friends. Told my professors, and later my bosses, about your column; how you were the gutsy, intelligent voice of the liberal minority in Oklahoma City; how you could so poignantly and humorously articulate the milestones and experiences of your personal life. I lugged your book across the country, from college in Chicago to summer jobs in D.C. and San Francisco, even to study abroad in France. But I never read it.

It's not that I was lazy. I was scared that it would make me love you more than I already do. And I just don't think that's a good idea, Mom.

Remember when you went on your first book tour? You held a reading in Washington D.C. at a women's book club. There were all of these high-powered career women in attendance, old friends from your days working in politics — powerful lobbyists, staunch feminists, shrewd businesswomen, lots of bold-faced names.

You read the column about missing your mother during the holidays. "Still Dead?" on page 69. "My mother has been dead for six years, and I think it's time for her to stop," you read. "Admittedly this has been an interesting phase, this dead part, but enough is enough."

I was so proud of you. But as I looked around the room, I noticed every single person there was crying. Hillary Clinton's future chief of staff wiped endless streams from her eyes. The finance reporter from the Washington Post sniffled and blew her nose.

I was terrified, realizing how much I was going to miss you too someday. "I have this to look forward to when you're gone?" I thought. "Gee, thanks Mom. This is going to be hell."

I knew you wouldn't be around forever, and maybe not even as long as other people's moms. You've had heart disease my entire life. Although, I don't remember knowing how serious it was until I was eight, when your heart started beating in the wrong rhythm. Your left ventricle is stiff; it doesn't pump very well. You walk slowly, stairs are hard, and you need to nap every day. But I've never, ever thought of you as sick. You just live too much.

I guess that's why I was so surprised when you told me last year that a reputable doctor suggested you put yourself on the list for a heart transplant.

"A heart transplant? Is he crazy?" I thought. No, no, that's not a good idea. She doesn't need a new heart. Maybe if this man knew my mother better he'd understand that.

If he had been at the party after my Bat Mitzvah he would remember that someone got on the microphone and asked how many people in the room considered themselves my mother's best friend. More than 30 people raised their hand, including, of course, my dad, and they all stared at each other laughing incredulously. This is a woman with a perfect heart.

Maybe if this doctor knew that my mom wants to jitterbug every time some good oldies come on, no matter where she is — crowded restaurant, state capitol, who cares. Of course you get tired after a minute or two and you have to sit down, but isn't it more important that you jumped up to dance in the first place? You've never been anything but vibrant, whole, bursting with enthusiasm for a day of impulse antique shopping, a wacky museum, a road trip for a slice of chocolate cake. Unconditional love comes as naturally to you as drawing air for breath, and you take joy from the smallest things in life. All of this comes from your heart.

But you've been tired recently, and it's been hard for you to write. Not long ago I called you to chat. You said, "I'm fine, just trying to get on with my day with this worthless sack of cellophane that's supposed to be pumping my blood."

Sack of cellophane? Worthless? No Mom, you're wrong. You're talking about the organ that keeps your husband, your children, your sister, your father, your friends, and your colleagues up and at 'em. How is it possible that this heart, which has comforted and supported so many people, struggles at its most basic function: keeping you healthy and alive? Why does the person I know with the most perfect heart have to trade it in?

You were asked to make a second and updated edition of your book about the same time you starting looking into heart transplant surgery. I still hadn't read your book, I was still afraid of loving you more. And with your name on a waiting list for a new heart, the day that I would start missing you could come much sooner than I expected.

When you asked me to write the foreword, I thought I was caught. "Don't worry that Bill Clinton wrote the one for my last book sweetie; you know me better than he does," you joked. You didn't know that I refused to find out what Bill Clinton had to say about you.

But it was time; I knew it. I wanted to write for you and I had to face this American Woman. I'm an adult now anyway, living in New York City, holding a job at a glossy magazine, paying bills, calling shots, making my way.

I read "Losing Bunny" on the subway to work – the column where you describe my misery after losing a beloved stuffed animal on an airplane in the weeks leading up to my Bat Mitzvah. As I nonchalantly elbowed my way through the rush hour crowd, I cursed you for announcing in print to all of Oklahoma City that I still cared about a stuffed bunny as a 12-year-old.

In the next few sentences of your story, I remembered the mix of embarrassment and alienation I felt when I had to explain to my non-

Jewish friends in Oklahoma exactly what they would be sitting through for two hours at our Temple as I recited my Torah portion. And finally, when you explained that Bunny's disappearance signaled my passage into adulthood, the disappearance of innocence, simplicity, and perfect love, I lost it. In public. Mashed between New Yorkers with numbing iPod buds stuck in their ears — you would have called them "over-stimulated by modern technology" — I cried on the Q train to Times Square.

Please keep writing, Mom. The sense of perspective, insight, and empathy that pours out of this book helps to fill holes created by life's most confusing, most upsetting and most challenging moments.

You have such a strong connection between your heart and your words, and they are both a gift to all of us.

December 2007

FOREWORD

Former President William J. Clinton

From the first time I met Pam Fleischaker, I knew she was comfortable with who she was and certain of her values.

We first met more than 30 years ago in Washington, D.C. I was a summer intern about to start law school. She was new to the East Coast, new to Washington and new to politics. She had taken a job with Common Cause, the citizens' lobby newly established to reform the already-broken campaign finance system.

Common Cause was a natural magnet for high-energy, ambitious, young progressives in the Nixon years. I had a lot of friends working at Common Cause, people with whom I had worked in various political campaigns, and it was at a party thrown by some of these friends that I met Pam. We have maintained our friendship over all the years since.

From our first conversation it was clear she was not your typical up-and-coming politico. She had worked as a fashion copywriter for Neiman-Marcus in Dallas, a job she loved, she was quick to add. So how did you end up at Common Cause? I asked. Mostly luck, she replied. She suspected she got the job because she told interviewers she loved to type and would do anything to help.

When I returned to Arkansas to run for public office, Pam remained in Washington, working in the vanguard of groups advancing congressional reform and assisting women running for political office.

In 1981, Pam left Washington and moved to Oklahoma with her family, but she remained involved in national politics. Our paths crossed often in the 1984 Mondale-Ferraro presidential campaign and again in 1988, in the Dukakis-Bentsen presidential effort. While we worked in more losing campaigns than I care to remember — including my own for Congress in 1974 — we shared a lot of common goals and good times.

In the Nineties, Pam began a new career as a columnist, writing for the Oklahoma Gazette in Oklahoma City.

In this collection taken from her weekly columns, you'll find her goading a reluctant Republican governor to enact sensible gun control laws, exposing the journalistic mediocrity of the city's powerful right-wing daily newspaper, and challenging those who would limit a woman's control over her body and destiny.

At the same time, she is a voice of reconciliation, appealing to those in her community — a predominantly white, conservative Christian community — to understand and be tolerant of those who are different, whether their difference is one of race, religion or sexual orientation.

One week Pam is upbraiding the self-appointed censors who would, in God's name, ban books from students' reading lists, and the next she is extolling the common virtues of the people in her community who still have time for simple expressions of decency.

And there is more: Pam revisiting the angst of her adolescence, recording her children's passages, extolling the virtues of foie gras, chocolate and shopping. Her range of commentary runs from Martha Stewart to Barry Bonds, from the First Amendment to the first date.

What makes this good reading is that Pam has an instinct for the unadorned, unvarnished truth. She speaks simply and honestly about her feelings. Add to that a large capacity for compassion, a rollicking sense of humor, stir in a little mischief, and you have my friend, Pam.

As you read these pieces, you'll find yourself thinking, "I remember feeling that way" and thinking that she's got it right. And you will find yourself laughing, laughing a lot.

Bill Clinton

February 2001

Still Lost and Found in Oklahoma

 compass is an appealing gadget, handsome in its casing, compact enough to stash in a pocket or leave dangling in the car for a reassuring glance. The engraved casement and scripted lettering can take me, imaginatively, onto the deck of a tall, many-masted ship with only the stars and my compass to guide me.

"North!" I might cry, eyes open wide, wind blowing through my hair. "We're going north!"

But LED dashboard instruments have taken the romance out of compasses, interstates can be followed almost blindly, and Google Maps leave little to imagine about getting from one place to another.

Yet like the rest of you, I really have no idea where I'm going, how long I'll stay or what's next. Compass or dashboard directionals aside, I am where I am.

In spite of a plan to "spend only three or four years in Oklahoma City," my husband and I are still here. (Husbands and politicians have something in common, don't you think? It's all promises, promises!) Twenty-five years later, we still enjoy the slow pace of life in the Heartland, minimal traffic congestion, great barbeque, good friends, and relatively clean air.

And I am still tilting at the windmills of this stubborn, often provincial culture, hoping to add constructively to my community and be of some value to those who live and work in it.

EVERYTHING OLD IS NEW AGAIN

"American Woman, Lost and Found in Oklahoma" was first published in May 2001, offering 45 of my opinion columns that appeared in the weekly Oklahoma Gazette between 1987 and 2000. It contained my perceptions about life in the Nineties.

For this revised edition, I set aside some dated pieces, kept what I hope are still-sturdy ones, and added some updates and new work written since 2001. I want to look at the ensuing years together, but I can't let go of the old. I hope you won't either.

Both the first book and this refreshed edition offer my observations, reflections and opinions about life — political, public and private. Those ten years — my sixth decade on this crazy globe — were the "middle years" for my family and me; a prosperous but ominous time in America (though only now, looking back, can we know that) and a difficult but promising era in the life of Oklahoma City.

The new pieces echo the changed, less-secure circumstances of our collective lives and some of the uncertainty that accompanies me into the next part of my life. Among other themes, I have added commentary about:

- America at war in Iraq and Afghanistan and the Bush administration's handling of that war in "Life During Wartime" and "Scoot, Scooter"
- Memorializing the lives lost in the 1995 bombing in Oklahoma City in "A Citadel in the City"
- Continuing conservatism in Oklahoma in "The Word on Oklahoma"
- Women leaders in "Jari in the House" and "A Man to do a Woman's Job"
- My own changed role in my family, "You're Fired" and my personal and professional campaigns in "Rescuing the Evidence" and "Free Speech and Flagpoles"

My true North is still discernible, though some help with direction — personally, politically, globally and in the cosmological order of things — is needed more than ever. I still use the compass, but I've noticed the needle getting a little shaky.

EVERYTHING CHANGES

On September 11, 2001, four passenger planes on America's East Coast were hijacked and brought down by 19 Islamic extremists in coordinated terrorist suicide attacks. Two of the planes were flown into two 110-story office towers in lower Manhattan known as the World Trade Center, destroying them and the seven other buildings in that landmark complex. Moments later another plane, similarly hijacked, crashed into the Pentagon outside Washington, D.C., and the fourth — thought to be headed for the White House — crash-landed in rural Pennsylvania. In all, 2,973 people were killed, including firefighters, rescuers, police officers, passengers on the planes and ordinary citizens working in or nearby the buildings.

These seemingly random assaults on our cities and citizens set events in motion that would lead to a new sense of insecurity in America and abroad; a realignment of our relationships with many other countries; and wars promulgated by our government on Iraq and Afghanistan which, at this writing, have resulted in the deaths of more than 4,000 Americans and an estimated one-million Iraqis and Afghans.

With that terrifying attack, Oklahoma City lost the monstrous distinction of being the site of the "greatest act of domestic terrorism on U.S. soil," a label attached to us after the bombing of the Murrah Federal Building here in April 1995, that killed 168 people.

Americans have moved on from Sept. 11, albeit with some lingering fears. We have learned to live with omnipresent security guards or law enforcement officers, intrusions into our most private records and communiqués, and the apparently permanent buzz of the threat of terror hovering over us.

News of the arrests or detainment of one suspected al-Qaida terrorist or another has become background noise for most of us. The so-called War on Terror is confusing, scattershot and in my view, unwinnable. The war in Iraq has brought a president to his knees, the Congress and the people it represents to the point of roiling frustration, and the economy to a tentative unsteadiness. Only the upcoming 2008 presidential election offers us any national diversion.

Optimistically, we have the prospect of change in our executive leadership. Remarkably for our country, we could elect a woman or an black president. In spite of growing indebtedness, America has great natural wealth, vigor and a lot of affluent individuals whose efforts to improve the economy and the lives of others are growing. Americans are ever-more philanthropic, hardworking, and engaged in public life, whether from the political right, left or center. Our democracy is alive and lively, and it still works, in spite of sputters and slow-downs.

Unfortunately, we struggle with immigration problems, unaffordable and unavilable health care for many, and an appetite for energy that threatens our safety — financially, militarily and environmentally. While we hope to make college education accessible to more in our society, college tuition is going up and student aid is going down. Most glaringly, primary and secondary education are still tragically under-serving our kids.

Globally, we are challenged by the rapid growth of both China and India, near-constant turmoil in the Middle East and Persian Gulf and the ever-present pestilence, famine and inhuman violence that seem to plague Africa. Climate changes threaten to affect all of these issues, and we are scrambling — in science, economics, manufacturing, government and in our policies — to step up to the provocations of our changed planet.

EVERYTHING'S GOIN' FINE

Post-Sept. 11 America and the planet on which it turns now sound, to me at least, like the cacophony of a louder and louder drum section, played under the swarm of swooping, hissing locusts. Yet all is pretty quiet here on the Western front. In fact, Oklahoma is almost tranquil in its comparative safety, impressive evolution, blue skies and still-hopeful frontier attitudes. We've always bucked the trends.

Since both the federal building bombing and the attacks of Sept. 11, Oklahoma City has emerged, like the mythic phoenix, with a rebuilt and greatly improved downtown, and we have addressed some of the inadequacies in our public schools. But first, we had to get past the bombing.

Timothy McVeigh, the Arizona man who delivered the bomb in a truck at the front of the federal building was tried, convicted and executed in June 2001. His accomplice, Terry Nichols, was tried in federal and state court and is serving a lifetime sentence in prison in Colorado. With those responsible for our losses gone, we heaved a collective sigh of relief here and began our turnaround.

The one-block square, $26 million Oklahoma City National Memorial & Museum was completed in 2001 and stands today as a beautiful, moving and educational tribute to the lives lost in the bombing. Visitors stand at the reflecting pool and try to imagine it. School children come through the museum and try to learn from it. Families of the victims still struggle with their losses. Oklahomans saw the worst hard times, and on we went.

OUT OF THE ASHES

Even before the bombing, elected civic and business leaders in Oklahoma City devised a plan called MAPS — Metropolitan Area Projects — whose broad goal was to rebuild much of downtown and revamp some of our public areas. By agreeing to a temporary one-cent sales tax, we built a new minor league ballpark in Bricktown and revitalized that former warehouse area with a canal, and bike and walking trails. We remodeled our convention center; updated facilities at the State Fairgrounds; built a new library, a new arena, a tourist trolley system and spiffed up our performing arts facilities.

Spurred on by this new-found pride — and unwilling to accept the hole left in the middle of town from the bombing — private money was raised, and an art museum was added downtown, a boat house was built on the newly-flowing river, shiny restaurants and hotels opened, and everything that was old in downtown Oklahoma City was new and alive again.

After MAPS saw its main projects to completion, Oklahoma City's citizens voted to tax themselves, again, to begin repairing our pubic schools, at least in terms of their physical plants, through a 10-year, $470 million program called MAPS for Kids.

Nationally and internationally the price of oil has risen and risen, causing pain at the gas pump for everyone who drives, but benefiting Oklahoma's still oil-dependent economy. We could afford to raise teachers' salaries across the state, build medical research facilities and we did.

As oil and gas prices rose, so did the fortunes of many independent energy-producing companies, always the state's strength. Devon Energy, today the largest independent oil & gas company in America, and Chesapeake Energy Corporation, the largest independent natural gas production company, have replaced older companies like Kerr-McGee and Conoco Phillips, and are both steered by philanthropic executives making waves in the power pools of the city. Still dependent on hydrocarbons, the state is finding its footing in the new world of wind energy and biofuels.

Financial and civic power in Oklahoma City, once vested in a few business leaders and the Gaylord family at the Oklahoma Publishing Co., has shifted. With the death of Edward Gaylord in 2003, the Oklahoman, still the state's largest newspaper, has softened its harsh editorial slant with somewhat more diverse voices and opinions. The new-generation Gaylord family is committed to Oklahoma City and its future in a more inclusive and positive way than their forefathers.

Yet with all of this growth, a gussied-up downtown, more philanthropy, new leadership and better-looking and better-run schools, we still have a lot to face and face up to.

The number of both Hispanic and Asian people in our city and metropolitan area has grown exponentially. We're richer because of these neighbors, but with rising health costs, schools bulging at the seams, and immigration laws unsettled, we have not yet absorbed these people into our town in a way that gives them an opportunity for productive lives. In fact, our state Legislature has passed laws that make the task of coping with these immigrants even more difficult. But that's another story.

As is the case in most suburban communities in America, the trappings of increased wealth are easy to spot in Oklahoma City, but the disparity between the lives of the rich and ultra-rich, and the lives of the working poor and impoverished is growing.

MY COMPASS

Family — surely the core of all of our lives, whatever its configuration may be — anchors me. I am lucky still to benefit from the wisdom of my 90-something father, to value the partnership of a 38-year marriage to a man I love and respect, and to feel pride, satisfaction and some relief at seeing my children grown, independent, working and playing hard.

I am no longer a regular commentator for the Oklahoma Gazette, though my work appears there occasionally. A laptop computer, cell phone and fax machine — my constant companions, though not my favorite ones — make it possible for me to work anywhere. With some technological freedoms and the emptying of my family nest, I spend more time away from Oklahoma City, enjoying bigger urban cities, following my now-grown kids from one adventure to the next (when they'll have me), or broadening my own world with travel.

Aging (and thank God, I am aging) is certainly not for sissies, as the cliché goes. Losing people you love to illness and death; watching your own body weaken or fade; accepting the limitations of aging. Coping with all of this with equanimity, grace and dignity is one tall order, but an order I hope to fill.

I keep writing because there is still much of this life to live — work to do, seeds to plant, wrongs to right, family to watch grow, friends to help and enjoy, chocolate to be eaten, and fun to be had.

I keep writing to join you in conversations that keep our minds lively, our eyes and minds open and our shopping sprees at a minimum.

I keep writing because the dissonant noise in America needs modulation, and in my own way as an American woman, I want my voice to be heard.

I keep writing because writers are losing heart, but I will not. (That's another other story.)

And I keep writing to help myself steady that shaky needle.

I do not promise, nor do I expect from you, easy answers, flexible joints, smooth skin, profound solutions, or an immediate end to the world's many woes. I do promise not to be a sissy about Whatever's Next, and I do promise to keep writing. I hope you'll join me.

Where you live is not important, wise people told me.

It's how you live that counts.

Still, I felt as though I was stepping off a cliff blindfolded as I readied myself in 1981 for a move from Washington, D.C. – where I had lived for nearly 12 years from my mid-twenties to mid-thirties – to Oklahoma City, my husband's hometown. Something I suspected about "place" worried me about this move.

I think place matters. I think that where you are has a lot to do with how you are. Where I would live – how it would look and smell, its energy, its taste, its history, its personality, its culture – all of that mattered to me, as I prepared to make a home in a town I would call my hometown.

Oklahoma City was then much like it is today. People were friendly and open. You could see all of the sky all of the time. The air was clear, the traffic was negligible. Lovely houses with big yards in nice neighborhoods were affordable and life was easy.

But for me, the change was a setback. I imagined I would never click with Oklahomans. In Washington, I had been schooled in assertive, activist, left-wing advocacy, thrived on it, in fact, and was afraid I would stick out like a sore, liberal thumb in laid-back Oklahoma.

Initially, I crossed paths with very few women who worked in Oklahoma City, even fewer who were passionate about their work. I sought out activists, but they were few and far between. Oklahoma's politics was full of good ol' boys (actually, good ol' men), corrupt county commissioners and a few bright lights, who, by then, were burning out. The media was, and is, The Daily Oklahoman, a big, domineering statewide newspaper run by a wealthy conservative family whose attitude seems to be keep 'em uninformed, barefoot and pregnant, and they won't ever want to leave the farm.

Yet it was in Oklahoma City that I eventually found deeply satisfying work and raised a strong, healthy family. I found as colleagues a group of smart, hardworking women and men dedicated to helping women and their families.

I always believed I was making a contribution in Washington, but it was hard to see. After months of killing work, my candidate always lost the White House, and those I'd help elect to Congress were swallowed up in the next election by another candidate with more money.

I began noticing — now with a more observant, less personal eye — what was available and what was missing in this city I was calling home, and I began writing about it, all of it. Politics, kids, husbands, being out when you wanted in, being in when it didn't work out. At first, I wrote mostly for myself and really to myself. Seeing it on paper helped me sort out what mattered and what didn't, where I was and why.

My point of view as a woman, a liberal, a Jew, an insider who always felt out, mattered to me more and more, particularly as that viewpoint was under-represented in the city.

I have tried to provoke and have certainly been provoked. I have tried to keep my topics, my writing and myself lively.

From the death of my much-loved mother, to my son's graduation, my daughter's coming of age and my husband's mid-life pursuits, I have tried to understand living by writing about it.

From the excitement and pride at seeing Bill Clinton, an old friend and political ally, elected President of the United States, to the confusion at his fall from grace, I have tried to understand national politics in America in the 21st century by writing about it.

From the perspective of a Jewish woman living in an overwhelmingly Christian community, I have tried to gain, and regain, my footing by writing about it.

From the inhumanity of a city commission's actions against its gay community to a terrifying act of domestic terrorism and destruction, I have tried to understand living in Oklahoma City by writing about it.

I have engendered enthusiasm and criticism for my positions. I have gotten phone calls, letters, e-mail and hate mail.

"Go for it, Pam!" one fellow wrote. "You're a light in the darkness."

"Go to hell, you damned liberal," wrote someone else.

Where you are does matter.

And here I am. Writing to myself, and for those like and unlike me from a place in the very middle of America.

I write from the place I hold as an American woman — a mother, a wife, an activist. I write from the extraordinary place of being an American at the turn of a fast-paced, high-tech century, an Oklahoman with an East Coast attitude and an outsider with an insider's moxie. In the frantic world of American political life, in the zigzagging but joyful refuge of my family and in the red earth of Oklahoma, I found a place.

May 2001

INTRODUCTION

Getting here from there

THE LAND OF NON-PERSPIRING BLONDES

A full-fledged Baby Boomer, I was born in 1946 to Bud and Dottie Mandell, who were struggling to make it in the postwar, rough and tumble oil and gas business in Texas. For the first 10 years of my life, my cheerful, optimistic and hardworking parents dragged my sister, Missy, and me all over the state from small, dusty towns that barely supported a truckload of oil field workers and a few "executives" (office boys), to bigger boom towns just beginning to shine, like Houston, Austin and Dallas.

I spent all of my adolescence in Dallas, sweltering in the heat, secure in what was a uniquely happy and close-knit family, but never feeling I fit in with the broader community.

All around me were pretty, pert blondes and big, beefy guys. In the way that only tortured adolescents can, I imagined these North Dallas girls lived in grand houses, wore clothes with the right labels, had sex with their boyfriends behind church social halls, and had tan, unblemished skin all year long. That was actually not just my imagination. That was North Dallas in the Sixties.

In this Land of Non-perspiring Blondes, I was a moody, big-featured, dark-haired Jewish girl who loved to dance and write. I liked conversation with smart, quick, nerdy boys, not driving around in the back of a hot, windy convertible lookin' for Bobby Lee and the rest of the defensive line. I had a few oddball friends who felt as out of place as I did, and I knew, as young as age 13, that this was the wrong place for me.

College at the University of Colorado, then at the University of Texas in Austin, was better. Finding some comfortable places for myself, I worked on the campus newspaper and became involved in student politics. Proudly, I marched to the steps of the Texas state Capitol against the war in Vietnam in 1968. Admiringly, I worked alongside my boyfriend (now husband) who was the brainy one in law school, the leader of the human-rights club.

Still, I felt I was pushing from the outside, never really to be in. Maybe it was the heat; maybe the attitudes; maybe it was my attitude. I could hardly wait to leave.

FINDING MY PLACE

At 22, when the brainy-boyfriend-husband, David, and I moved to Washington, D.C. (for his job, of course, but I quickly found one), I came alive.

With luck, I landed a post with a group of young political activists working for Common Cause, a citizens' lobby committed to election law and campaign finance reform. We — oh, how I loved using that word we — worked to pass an amendment giving 18-year-olds the right to vote and brought lawsuits to make campaigning and lobbying more open and above board. And like almost every other activist group in Washington in the late Seventies, we proudly and aggressively opposed the war in Vietnam.

My boss and mentor then — and my good friend now — was Anne Wexler, a then 40-something woman who had been a key player in several Democratic presidential and U.S. Senate campaigns. Like a powerful incarnation of the Pied Piper, she convinced her small staff of young reformers and political organizers that we could, and should, do anything we believed in.

Our band of earnest advocates eventually spread out in two Democratic presidential campaigns — Ed Muskie's and, when that failed, George McGovern's. We worked ridiculously hard, because we believed the political system needed us, because we were ambitious and thought we could change at least some part of the world, because we were young and because it was fun. Really fun.

BIG SHOTS AT 25

I felt I had finally found my place — outside government but inside the world of political activism. For the next 10 years I continued working for political advocacy groups against the war in Vietnam, for the right to choose abortion, for ratification of the Equal Rights Amendment, for public financing of elections, and for women running for public office.

I was involved in Democratic campaigns like Geraldine Ferraro's first bid for Congress in New York; Bill Clinton's unsuccessful bid for Congress from Arkansas; Tom Harkin's first run for Congress from Iowa; Barbara Mikulski's first race for the U.S. Senate from Maryland.

On one particularly wild ride in 1972, my husband and I, my sister, Wexler and her husband Joseph Duffey, and no more than about 10 other 20ish-year-olds, put on a national Democratic issues convention in Louisville, KY, with 2,000 delegates, 500 members of the national press corps, and seven Democratic presidential candidates. We thought we were running the world.

Chutzpah? You bet. In over our heads? Certainly. But we were passionate, committed and willing to work ourselves to the bone. At 25, we were big shots.

In those years in Washington, I cut my teeth, professionally, on helping public servants who did good, honest work in politics. That system has gone sour for most, but it never went sour for me.

I knew then, and still know today, men and women in both political parties and at all levels of government who work hard and with integrity for the public they serve. By dint of my own abilities and my willingness to work, I finally understood the satisfaction and the responsibilities of being an insider. And I have not lost my faith in America or its madcap systems of lawmaking and governing.

DO I GET A TURN?

By the time I was 30, I wanted a family and a less frenetic pace. I took a job as an associate political producer for CBS News in Washington, D.C. during the election period of 1976 and thrived again.

I saw candidates, issues and politicians from the other side, from the perspective of the media covering their campaigns. I wrote for correspondents and producers and loved it.

Our son, Joey, was born the next year, and while I stayed in the political media game in Washington, directing my professional energy toward electing women in both parties to office, my priorities had changed. I wanted to be home more and tried, with uneven success, to balance my growing professional life with the needs of my growing child. It was, and is, the hardest work I've ever done.

In 1981, my husband decided to leave his career as an environmental attorney in Washington and return to take up the reins of a family oil and gas business in Oklahoma. For two years, while our son grew from 2 to 4, my husband commuted between his business in Oklahoma City and our home and family in Washington. I kept "doing politics," taking care of our son and trying to be supportive of David's absences. Lots of people had commuting marriages, we said to each other; we'd manage, too.

But in fact, it was awful — an impossible way to conduct a relationship and no way to run a family or two careers. So I packed up and we moved.

TWO PLACES AT ONCE

Now I had one foot in Oklahoma, the other in Washington, and was looking for the best way to bridge the gap for myself.

The right to choose safe and legal abortion was seriously at risk in Oklahoma in the early Eighties, and I immediately saw ways I could help.

For many years, I worked for Planned Parenthood of Central Oklahoma, lobbying in the state Legislature and growing the ranks of supporters in the central part of the state. When I was seven months pregnant with our daughter, I stood before a state Senate committee and persuaded enough members to vote against a severe abortion restriction to defeat the measure.

In Washington, D.C., while the issue is attacked legally and through national policy, it is always at a distance. Weeks of work with the staff of a congressional committee might change one word in one line of a bill about family planning funds, only to be used as a political ploy to defeat some other issue. Presidential vetoes and the U.S. Supreme Court are the battlegrounds for fighting for abortion rights at that level.

In Oklahoma, the hostility toward those of us advocating the preservation of this legal procedure was, and is, palpable. It takes more than hard work and dedication to buck the majority in the Bible Belt — it takes moxie, and I am proud to say, I knew how to use it.

In slow-moving, stubborn Oklahoma, my ability to persuade one person to vote no on one legislative committee made the difference in preserving personal medical decisions for thousands of women.

Work, career and passion finally merged for me in the Heartland, bringing a sense of accomplishment I thought I'd left behind for good.

Someone reminded me recently that life is not one thing after another. It's the same damn thing over and over again.

So it goes with family planning and abortion rights. That fight has to be fought over and over again. I was glad to be in it then, and I'm glad now.

HOW YA GONNA KEEP 'EM DOWN ON THE FARM?

In spite of the gratifying work I was doing in Oklahoma, I missed the energy and excitement of national politics.

So in the national election of 1984, barely retired from nursing our newborn, Emily, I worked for and traveled with Geraldine Ferraro, the Democratic nominee for vice president and the first woman on a presidential ticket. A woman was running. It was an historic, groundbreaking event and I wanted to be part of it. I bunked in with my friends Wexler and Duffey, and worked as Ferraro's liaison with women and women's organizations, a job that was exhilarating, important, fun and exhausting.

This time, I was the weekend commuter with two kids at home. After we lost that election — my Democrats were batting 0 for 3 — I came home, both to my family and Oklahoma Planned Parenthood.

I geared up again for Mike Dukakis' race for president in 1988, commuting between Boston and Oklahoma. I worked in the campaign's communications office, writing the candidate's responses and trying to persuade the media — yes, spin — to see and report the campaign our way.

I enjoyed this process, a new one for me, different from my feminist-driven legislative advocacy work. I was fascinated with the reporter's difficult task of sorting out the facts from the line skillfully crafted by a campaign, and with the campaign staff's difficult task of packaging and sending a candidate's image, positions and responses. However, unlike Ferraro's "first woman" campaign and my privileged role in that, candidate Dukakis wasn't up to the task and neither was I. As ever, I enjoyed working with a team of bright, committed political co-workers, led by Susan Estrich, the campaign's able manager and my good friend. But on the campaign trail, neither the candidate nor I seemed to know what city we were in or why. We lost, and I came home.

Four presidential campaigns, a lot of liberal doing good, two kids and a husband who supported it all but struggled to keep the family's equilibrium. I was finally getting some perspective.

The balancing act between career and family was killing me. Presidential politics was for young people who could live on powdered sugar donuts and liked the game more than the reasons for playing. My kids needed me, and I needed them. While I still didn't fit into any obvious role in Oklahoma, I was ready to be somewhere I could call home.

HANGING MY HAT

Back in Oklahoma City, I threw myself into volunteer work. I served Planned Parenthood on its board; I participated in a leadership training course for the city; I helped Democrats run for office and was appointed to the city's short-lived Human Rights Commission. I was always drawn to the outsider's fight, the rights of the individual, the defense of the exiled, the cause of the underdog, not a point of view easily or often voiced in Oklahoma City.

"You need a woman's voice on this paper," I said to my friend Randy Splaingard, the editor of the Oklahoma Gazette in the Eighties. "And I don't mean pie recipes and costume-making," I added, although I have happily written about both.

I meant writing about things traditionally done by men in Oklahoma, like politics and lobbying, religion and reform, and being taken seriously for it.

AN ALTERNATIVE FOR ME AND OKLAHOMA CITY

The Oklahoma Gazette is an alternative weekly newspaper launched in 1979 by owner and publisher Bill Bleakley. His worthwhile goal was to provide a compilation of arts and entertainment events, in-depth news reporting, good humor, good writing and an open forum for ideas. This kind of paper was, and still is, sorely needed in a news black hole left by the existing daily paper, The Daily Oklahoman, and was met with tremendous enthusiasm and success.

In 1987, I began writing a weekly commentary column for the Gazette called "At Liberty." Eventually, I joined the staff of the paper as senior associate editor and writer. Today, the Gazette's circulation is

56,000, and it is, without question, the only beacon of journalistic light in central Oklahoma.

For 14 years — as I raised a family, remained involved in my community and confronted my own transformation from young, headstrong activist to older and wiser activist — I have written for the Gazette, supported by tremendous intellectual and artistic freedom. I worked with other excellent writers, conceptualizing and editing stories alongside Mike Easterling, an editor and comrade-in-arms whose judgment, integrity, work ethic and keen eye for fairness are unexcelled in our region. His support, encouragement and respect made it possible for me to grow as a writer and editor, as well as make a contribution to our community.

The paper and its role in Oklahoma City have been my outlet and my inlet, my way of thinking out loud. I have written, re-written and published the column for more than 10 years. This collection represents only a few from those years, with some columns presented as they were originally published and others given background or explanation in a prologue or epilogue. The date under each column's title was its original publication date in the Gazette; the prologues and epilogues were written for this book.

The columns — a home site for some, bird-cage liner for others — have given me, and I hope my neighbors in Oklahoma City, the liberty to think, write and talk about public and private issues. They have given me a new career, a way to reinvent myself, and a chance to write about culture and cuisine, people and politics, family and feminism, things serious and things, at times, very silly.

May 2001

ONE

PROMS, PENNY-LOAFERS AND OTHER PRIVILEGES

PROM NIGHT

MAY 1988

964. Beatles. Big Hair. Bourbon on the Rocks. Boys, boys, boys, boys, boys.

My prom night approaches, and I don't have A Date. It's amazing that I'm actually willing to admit it, though I feel sure that everyone in the Lone Star state has noticed. My best friend, Valerie, knows for sure, because she doesn't Have One either and is likewise consumed with The Shame Of It All. My parents certainly know because my usual adolescent obnoxiousness has reached a new high.

I am one tormented teen.

"Don't worry, honey," my mom says lovingly, but oh, so naively. "There's still a month left. Someone will call."

I glare at both my parents. How can two people be so useless?

The weeks go by. I stalk the halls at school, sizing up any hopefuls but trying not to look too desperate. I feel an enormous arrow must be dangling above my head, following me everywhere, pointing down at me as if to say, "Her! Her! There's one! No one has asked Her yet!"

Now, one week to go and still no calls. I closet myself in my bedroom and stare at the phone which has grown so large it seems to fill every inch of my pink-and-white gingham French-provincial room. And speaking of pink princesses, they all have dates, every last one of them.

"You and Valerie could go together," suggests my mom, leaping years ahead with a very liberated idea. But I was horrified at one more reminder that she really didn't get it.

Things have changed for some prom-goers, and many girls do go with a girlfriend or in groups. Some brave souls even go alone. Their courage astounds and delights me.

But here in Oklahoma City at Putnam City West High School, things actually got worse for a while. For several years, they had an unfortunate policy that required students to attend the prom "with a member of the opposite sex" or not at all.

Had I waited for someone of the opposite sex to pluck me from the vast garden of gorgeous blossoms, I would surely have withered on the vine.

Now that 30 years have passed, one P.C. West student took on the issue, claiming the policy infringed on her rights. You bet it does. I'd say it infringes on her whole adolescence. Asking and fearing the dreaded response, "Well, uh, I don't think . . . ," has always been a painful position for both boys and girls, so why force them into it?

We tell them to grow up, be independent, accept responsibility for your own actions, resist the temptations of the crowd and think for yourself — except, of course, in this small matter of your social life and its pinnacle event. In this case, what you do must depend entirely on someone else. Someone else of the opposite sex, yet. Either put yourself heavily on the line, the message is, or stay home. This policy could create an entire generation of agoraphobics who can't leave the house unless they get The Big Call and a corsage.

But you must be dying to hear the end of my story. I simply could not stay home and watch one more Bing Crosby movie with my dad, so I took matters into my own hands.

"Ricky?" I said when my friend in Fort Worth answered the phone.

"Would you be able to come over — I lived in Dallas — and go to my prom with me?"

Ricky Rapfogel. A nice enough guy when he wasn't buried in Kafka or the College Board Study Guide. His dad would let him use the car. He looked perfectly fine. He could be talked into dancing from time to time, and he wasn't that much shorter than I was.

At first, silence from Ricky's end. Then, "What do I have to wear?"

"A tux." I wanted to add "dummy," but some wise voice told me to curb my sarcastic tongue for once.

"Sure," he said. "Why not? See you."

Saved, once again, by a member of the opposite sex.

EPILOGUE

Someone related to Ricky Rapfogel's mother has a cousin who has a niece whose daughter is married to a guy whose sister-in-law lives in Oklahoma City.

Still with me?

She sent Ricky a copy of this column from the Oklahoma Gazette and Ricky tracked me down. We spent 45 minutes on the phone, catching up on years of what's-what, and who married who and who's kids are where. Now we exchange greeting cards and occasional phone calls, and I'm glad to have him back.

He's a psychiatrist in a big city in the Midwest, and when I started blathering all of the above to him, he wisely said we shouldn't overcomplicate the cultural and developmental aspects of it. Mostly, he said, he'd been glad to go with me to the Hillcrest High School prom in Dallas 36 years ago.

"Really?" I replied, still incredulous.

"Yeah."

That Ricky.

"It was a lot of fun." he said.

🌹

READY OR NOT

NOVEMBER 1989

He was riding his bike home, I was out for my afternoon walk, and our paths happened to cross. Since he was juggling a lot — books, a basketball, his costume for the school play — his bike swerved and bumped into me if I walked too close. But if I kept a comfortable distance, it was a nice journey and we both enjoyed the company.

My son is nearly 13 and soon he will become Bar Mitzvah, an important and joyous ritual in our Jewish faith. It means "keeper of the commandments" and is a time when Jewish young men are invited, and expected, to share the responsibilities and privileges of the adult community.

For the first time, they are asked to read the Torah — God's laws or the first five books of the Old Testament — before the entire community and are given the responsibility for keeping them. Not until age 13 is it believed a child is able to accept this awesome task. Learning to read Hebrew and understanding the meaning of the prayers is hard work. Before 13, it's just too hard. But now, at the threshold of manhood, it's time to begin.

"Begin" because it is only a beginning. He is not a boy one day and a man the next. He is not oblivious to the law one day and mindful of it the next. He is beginning to become a man, beginning to understand the ancient teachings of his family's faith and beginning to struggle with his own choices.

And I am just beginning to accept his coming manhood. I cannot truthfully say, "Why, it was just yesterday when my baby boy...," because it wasn't. A lot of territory has been covered in 13 years.

He is an active, intense, super-charged guy with a warm heart, a gentle spirit and a pack of talent. He grabs life — usually in the form of a base-ball, soccer ball, balletic leap or basketball — and wrestles with it, kicks it, slams it, practices it and finally conquers it. His path is not yet a smooth one.

My instinct, as his mother, is to try to smooth the way, slow the pace, intercept the fast pass and wind down the pitch. If I help him with the responsibilities and rough spots, I sometimes reason, look at how much more he'll enjoy the rewards.

But I cannot slow him down, nor would I. Time is flying, and so is he. As he races past me into adulthood, I can only be there, and not too close at that. If I keep my distance, maybe he'll keep bumping into me.

Just step back and watch, mom, even when he fumbles, overshoots, pitches wild or falls. His job is to begin to accept the responsibilities of his coming manhood, in Judaism and in all of life. Your job is to let him.

Because ready or not, here he comes.

MOM'S RIGHT

MAY 1990

S o sure was my mother that black-suede penny loafers would ruin my feet, I was forbidden to wear them.

Every other seventh-grade girl at Ben Franklin Junior High in Dallas — that's 250 girls, 500 feet — had at least one pair. They were the thing that assured your status, marking you as "in" or, in my case, "out." I never owned a single pair.

Instead, I wore black and white saddle oxfords. They were, my mother sensibly proffered, sturdy and reasonably priced, and they provided excellent support.

I was so mortified, so unconsolably miserable, that she finally but only partially relented. I was allowed to wear brown-leather penny loafers. They passed the "sturdiness" test, more or less.

I have finally forgiven my mother. I have also finally figured out her real motive for this uncharacteristically inflexible edict. The concern for my growing arches was a ruse. What really bugged her was the boring conventionality that pervaded both the Fifties and the instincts of adolescents. She'd have probably let me wear rubber flip-flops if I'd just thought of it myself — anything, but the same ol' black-suede penny loafers.

But it's the only time in all of my teen-age years I remember her being stuffy and stubborn, giving me the right message the wrong way. In fact, my teen years were better than most because of my mom.

While other mothers were angered or terrorized by the moodiness, surliness or other horriblenesses of their teen-agers, mine relaxed. She thought my sister and I were fun and funny. She puttered around, comfortably drifting in and out of our activities, always encouraging, always positive.

8

When we lost sleep over our too-curly hair, she giggled. If we became hysterical about some thick-necked quarterback who never called, she hugged, sympathized and diverted. If we moaned about our awkward bodies, she praised and admired.

She thought we were wonderful and smart and we believed her. We still do.

It's been her best act, steering kids down the slippery slope of adolescence and onto the launch paid of adulthood.

She drew the line at some things, but it was a curving line, deftly making room for our unpredictable needs and natures. She brought sensitivity and good humor to the raising of teenagers, and I hope I can, too.

Empathizing with the insecurity that blankets my teen, I try to find that curvy line between reinforcing what is special about him and helping him fit in. And let me wow you with my tolerance.

I have no problem with sloppy T-shirts, buzz hair cuts or most rap music. I don't even hyperventilate anymore when I see body piercings. But I draw the line at pumped-up, souped-up basketball shoes, worn with laces untied and costing more than the mayor makes in a month.

Besides, Mom's right. Everyone's wearing them.

EPILOGUE

My mother, Dorothy (Dottie) Mandell died in 1990. A fine musician and actor herself, I hate to think what she'd have thought of rap artists. Good natured and unconventional, open-minded and certainly no cultural elite, still, she had her standards. "What's with his miserable mouth?" she'd have probably said about Eminem. "Yuck! Who needs it?!" Who needs it, indeed.

A BIRTHDAY GIFT

DECEMBER 1994

ou can do a lot when you're 18. Even legally. Maybe not wisely, but at least legally.

You can eat too many quarter-pounders with cheese, drive around in a gyrating car that sounds like a base woofer on wheels, have sex and use contraceptives (hopefully) without your parents even knowing, wear a baseball cap forward, backward or any which way you want.

You can watch lots of ESPN, play real sports or dress in camouflage and shoot at other people with paint guns; you can make the honor roll or blow off studying; burn CDs or burn rubber; get a job, lose a job, go to college, stay home.

You can be tried in a court of law as an adult. (You already have that honor in Oklahoma when you're only 13 and the charge is murder.) You can enter into some legal contracts and you can even get married. You can — must, in fact — register for the draft, and you can die for your country.

At 18 in America, you have reached your "majority," a term, according to Black's Law Dictionary, that means "full age; legal age, the age at which, by law, a person is entitled to the management of his own affairs ... " or hers, I hope. Dear Mr. Black probably just didn't know any women of majority.

My son is 18 this week.

Now he is, legally and officially, entitled to manage his own affairs and to enjoy his civic rights, assuming there are any left for him to enjoy after the Republicans have a go at it.

I told him I was taking him out for a little birthday surprise on his lunch break. I know he was hoping to test drive a new Beamer or fit bindings on new skiis, but when he figured out we were headed for the nearest agency to register him to vote, he looked at me and smiled.

He knows I see this as a gift; indeed, a very valuable gift. If not a gift, it is a privilege afforded too few people in the world and not used by nearly enough of those who have it.

The right to vote doesn't come in the bottom of a Cracker Jack box. It's part of the Constitution of the United States. Every man and woman who served in every war the United States has been in has liked the gift well enough to fight and sometimes die for it.

The right to vote was not automatically included in the Constitution for everyone. Blacks and former slaves couldn't vote until the ratification of the 15th Amendment in 1870. Before 1920 it was just a guy thing; women weren't given the right to vote until the 19th Amendment was ratified.

And prior to ratification of the 26th Amendment in 1971, these funky 18-year-olds with their joyous hearts, TV-minds and risky lifestyles couldn't vote, either. Now they can, but they don't. Forty percent fewer 18- to 24-year-olds voted in the last election [1] than the rest of those eligible, and the reasons, while not certain, can be pretty well guessed at.

"Why bother?" they ask. I may be responsible and use my vote, but elected officials are behaving less and less responsibly. Indeed, today's teen-ager has seen our government contribute little to progress for the good, seeing instead the growing cynicism of their parents and older adults about their own lives and the government's capacity to impact them.

He or she sees too much violence, too much fear, too much hatred, too much stress, too many options, too much television, too much self-seeking and too little generosity. She or he has probably had too little education — especially civic and community education — too little respect for public service, too little respect for and from adults.

The pull of cynicism is great, so you may think this is all a lot of stupid Sixties stuff about saving the world. It's not.

---

[1] This refers to the mid-term Congressional and gubernatorial elections of 1994. In the 2000 presidential elections, the rate of participation in this age group was even smaller.

11

One vote can matter. King Charles I of England was beheaded after a vote of 68–67; the Alaska Purchase of 1867 was ratified by just one vote; and Adolph Hitler was elected leader of his party in 1923 by a margin of just one vote.

I'm not so naïve to think my one vote, or yours, will change the direction of our country. Nor am I so irresponsible to throw away my one vote, the gift won for me with the blood, sweat and tears of our forefathers.

At the conclusion of the Constitutional Convention, Benjamin Franklin was asked, "What have you wrought?"

He answered, " … a Republic, if you can keep it."

Democracy, dudes, is not a spectator sport. Your vote is your voice.

Use it.

Register, vote and happy birthday.

EPILOGUE

In the 2000 presidential election, after protracted squabbling, vote recounting, lawsuits filed and finally the involvement of the U.S. Supreme Court, George W. Bush was declared the winner of Florida's electoral votes by winning only approximately 600 votes more than Democratic candidate Al Gore out of more than 100 million cast. If 600 votes can make the difference, it becomes easier to see that every vote does count. On the other hand, the legal and public relations battles for the decisive Florida vote, a not-so-pretty picture that went on for weeks after election day, might have been enough to turn off even the most patriotic voter. Let's hope not.

LIFE DURING WARTIME
OCTOBER 2006

 At a closing performance earlier this month at Manhattan's legendary music venue CBGB, Oklahoman Victoria Liedtke performed a cover of Talking Heads' song "Life During Wartime," putting special emphasis on the line, "We're tapping phone lines, I know that ain't allowed." The 20- and 30-something crowd went wild to the obvious reference to the current administration's secret wiretapping policy.

The energy was palpable, I'm told, vibrating with protest about at least one thing that motivates young people, "Man, get off my phone line!"

But where's that energy on Election Day? Do 18- to 29-year-olds vote? Are those votes well informed?

From a 23-year-old law student: "It's hard to feel connected to any particular ballot when you are young and transient – so no matter how interested you are in the national scene – you still may not feel particularly excited about your own vote."

"Activism isn't as trendy as it was when your generation was involved," said my daughter, an aspiring magazine writer in Manhattan. "And besides, I can't even pay my taxes let alone figure out how the government ought to spend them."

These responses elicit a groan from me. For baby boomers raised on protest marches, storming university buildings, working in the civil rights and feminist movements – just voting isn't enough.

But voting is a start, and the news there is hopeful. In the 2004 presidential election, the rate of eligible 18-to-29-year olds who voted was 49 percent nationally, nine points more than in 2000 and the highest rate since 1992. In Oklahoma that year, it was 45 percent.

In part because of an enormous expenditure of time and money in search of every new vote — and because it was a polarizing presidential election — both parties and many nonprofit groups registered young voters in 2004.

In the 2006 midterm election, fewer people of every age likely will vote. Still, it's an election that could change the direction of the country if power shifts from Republicans to Democrats in either house of Congress or away from the Democrats in our state Senate. And young voters know something's up.

Hooked up online, on blogs and on late-night television, they may not be deep into the issues, but they do pay attention to information and know where to get it.

"This generation of Ys is idealistic and concerned, compared to the Xers, who tend to be pessimistic and detached," reported The Washington Post quoting Peter Levine of the voter data-gathering group CIRCLE.

What do they care about? College affordability, jobs and the economy; Iraq, insurance and privacy questions.

After his early foray into political campaigning, my son, now 30, is a sports video producer, also in Manhattan, but he's still very interested in politics.

"I think the best way to reach my age group," he told me, "is through entertainment."

Many agree. MTV's Rock the Vote recently partnered with Facebook to encourage online voter registrations; DJs in Chicago threw a dance party to prompt voter participation; and in Oklahoma City, Wayne Coyne of the famed music group, Flaming Lips, drew a huge crowd on behalf of state senate candidate Andrew Rice.

This entertainment focus might explain the popularity of "The Daily Show" as a primary news source for these kids. Jon Stewart delivers real news, which is often bad news, but it's almost always dished out with hilarity. I guess his viewers figure if they can't fix it, at least they can laugh about it.

And last, in the words of one up-and-coming 17-year-old activist, "Sure I'll vote. I want somebody to know where I stand. It's a warning before I rise up in armed rebellion."

The voting, the verdict on whether they vote — and maybe the rebellion — are Nov. 7. Show up.

Epilogue

The news about young voters in the 2006 mid-term congressional election was good. Eighteen- to 29-year-olds voted in the largest numbers in at least 20 years, energized largely by the Iraq war.

- *About 24 percent of Americans under 30, or at least 10 million young people, voted. A survey of these new voters conducted for George Washington University looked primarily at their motivation for going to the polls.*

- *58 percent said they talked with family or friends before the election.*

- *43 percent said the most important issues to them when deciding who to vote for was the war in Iraq.*

- *35 percent voted for Republicans; 50 percent for Democrats.*

- *And finally, young voters reported they decided to vote because someone from a campaign asked them to, often with a phone call or an in-person visit.*

We used to call that retail politics — discussion, conversation, an exchange of ideas — and the news it still works is music to the ears of this old-fashioned grass-roots political organizer.

TWO

OK BY ME

OUR TOWN

APRIL 1995

PROLOGUE

A few minutes before 9 a.m. on April 19, 1995, Timothy McVeigh, a young man with a deep and burning hatred for the U.S. government, drove a rented, yellow Ryder truck east on Northwest Fifth Street in downtown Oklahoma City. He parked the truck in front of the main entrance to the nine-story Alfred P. Murrah Federal Building, got out and left the truck.

At 9:02 a.m., a 5,600-pound fertilizer and fuel bomb, placed in the back of the truck by McVeigh, exploded as intended, demolishing the front half of the office building from the ground up. After days of clearing away the rubble and debris and rescuing those who survived, the death toll reached 168, including 19 children.

The bomb went off just as people were settling into their desks in the federal building and just as parents were taking their infants and children into the day-care center on the first floor of the building.

The building housed offices for a long list of federal agencies, including the Social Security Administration; the Bureau of Alcohol, Tobacco and Firearms; the Secret Service; Immigration and Naturalization; the U.S. Department of Agriculture; and U.S. Department of Housing and Urban Development.

Hundreds of doctors, nurses and rescue personnel began immediately setting up triage and care units on site which funneled the injured into other medical settings at area hospitals.

Fire fighters and police – from Oklahoma City, surrounding towns and even from states beyond Oklahoma – sprang into action, digging for injured victims, clearing debris, pulling bodies from the wreckage. The recovery effort continued into the following month as the final three bodies were pulled from the rubble.

Religious groups established shelters throughout the city for refuge, both physical and spiritual. Social workers, psychologists, psychiatrists and counselors spread out between various sites established to comfort victims and their families. Food banks made supplies available to rescue workers; the American Red Cross began its highest level of relief aid; money poured in from individuals and organizations wanting to help; and from all parts of the city and state, individuals arrived in downtown Oklahoma City, lining up to help.

McVeigh was picked up on an unrelated offense, just hours after the bombing, near the small town of Perry, Okla.

That same year, a federal grand jury indicted McVeigh and his friend, Terry Nichols, for murder and for the bombing conspiracy. The pair were prosecuted in federal court in Denver for the murders of the eight federal law enforcement officers who died in the explosion.

McVeigh was convicted and sentenced to death. Nichols, who helped mix the bomb and finance the bombing, was convicted of involuntary manslaughter and given a sentence of life in prison. At both trials, federal prosecutors were aided by the testimony of Michael Fortier, a one-time friend of McVeigh's.

Prosecutors were able to prove the pair were motivated, in part, by the fiery end to a standoff between U.S. law enforcement officials and the residents of the Branch Davidian Compound in Waco, Texas, that occurred on the same day, April 19, in 1993.

he land is flat here — flat, red and hard like the rusty-colored granite that was, until last week, the composition of the Alfred P. Murrah Federal Building in the middle of downtown Oklahoma City.

It's so flat that from some vantage points far away, you can even see the building which now looks as if someone reached down with a jagged pruning hook and gouged out the center. This building was, until last week, the workplace of about 500 government employees and a safe haven for 30 children sheltered in an on-site day-care center.

It's so flat and dry and dusty here you worry that maybe this eroded red earth, this endless gritty wind and this dry, dry land has made all of us who live here hard and dry and brittle, too. Daily, you steel yourself to the wind and the dust; you try to appreciate the pace of an easy, every-day life where nothing fantastic ever happens, but nothing very terrible happens either.

You accept that our city will never host the Olympics. You know Broadway producers won't suddenly bring great theater here. You know Michael Jordan or Nolan Ryan will never play here, that you won't see Hollywood stars eating at fabulous restaurants or world leaders arriving for a summit.

If something really significant did happen here, you wonder, would we be hard and dry and dusty in its face, too?

But those were yesterday's questions, before my children heard and felt an explosion sitting in their classrooms four miles away from downtown, before my husband and his co-workers felt their 33-story building convulse, before hundreds of people — too many of them babies and young children — would be counted as dead, buried beneath that dry granite. Now all that hardness has turned to dust, and hundreds more people roam the streets, hospitals and make-shift shelters desperate to find family or friends on a list of "treated and released."

Since I have lived here, I have been afraid that this land and its dull, near-barren character had eroded our energy, our ambition and our spirit. But that was yesterday, before our under-funded, previously criticized police department responded with speed, efficiency and calm. That was before thousands of people lined the streets to give blood within just two hours of the explosion.

That was before hundreds of doctors, nurses and medical personnel came, unbidden, from towns like Waurika, Seminole, Tulsa, Shawnee and Choctaw to lend a hand. That was before our fire department launched a rescue effort far beyond anything they had done before and far beyond anything many cities could handle at all.

Within a few hours of the bomb's explosion, we had more volunteers, more donations of food, water, blankets, medical equipment and counseling than we needed.

We had a city-wide media effort that delivered fast, accurate and helpful information – unsensationalized and trustworthy. We had elected officials who, a week before, were sniping at each other over nothing, now standing arm-in-arm giving us reasons for optimism. We had a system of hospitals, doctors and nurses so generous and competent there was, quite literally, one doctor available for every single patient brought to them.

Here is what I have learned this week about the people who live simply and quietly in Oklahoma City. We are responding, not only to the worst act of terrorism to occur in the United States, but to events of much greater significance – one man's life, one woman's mother, one neighbor's friend; each person's toil, each family's bond, each child's future.

HEAT

AUGUST 1990

H eat ... sizzling heat ... Promethean heat ... prickly heat ... blinding heat ... The Long Hot Summer. "We're having a heat wave, a tropical heat wave ..." disco inferno, Burn Baby Burn ... too hot to handle ... Pease-porridge hot ... hot and bothered ... hot tamale ... hot potato ... hot dog ... hot tempered ... hot headed.

"It's too hot, too hot baby, better run for shelter, better run for shade" ... if you can't stand the heat, get out of the kitchen.

"Here comes the sun, little darling" ... Don't just stand there and let the sun burn a hole in ya ... In the Heat of the Night ... like a raisin in the sun ... "For he shall be like the heat in the desert, and shall not see when good cometh."

Some Like it Hot ... Good Day Sunshine ... "Come on, baby, light my fire" ... There'll be a hot time in the old town tonight ... in the house of the rising sun ... red hot 'n' blue ... hotsy-totsy ... hotcakes ... hot diggity dog ... "Surprised was I with sudden heat which made my heart glow"... "Sunshine came softly through my window today ..."

"You are my sunshine, my only sunshine, you make me happy when skies are gray."

"Not snow, no, or rain, nor heat, nor night keeps them from accomplishing their appointed courses with all speed" ... The queen of hearts she made some tarts, all on a summer's day.

"Shall I compare thee to a summer's day?" But it's too darned hot. ... Mad dogs and Englishmen go out to the midday sun ... "hot town summer in the city, back 'o my neck gettin' dirty and gritty" ... "moral equivalent of war; analogous, as one might say, to the mechanical equivalent of heat."

"Goodness, gracious, great balls of fire!" ... The Towering Inferno ... and in the metro area, sunny and hot again today ... "and they whose hearts are dry as summer dust burn to the socket" ... "one draught above heat makes him a fool, the second mads him and a third drowns him" ... "Double, double, toil and trouble, fire burn and cauldron bubble" ... up in smoke ... "We didn't start the fire; it was always burnin' since the world's been turnin'."

"Heat cannot of itself pass from a colder to a hotter body" ... just add hot water and serve.

" ... or art thou a dagger of the mind, a false creation proceeding from the heat-oppressed brain."

A CITADEL IN THE CITY

APRIL 2005

In the center of our city there is a monument to those killed in the 1995 federal building bombing. It is meant to preserve the memory of lives lost there; to offer compassion to families and friends who will always feel those losses; and to encourage reflection about how, or if, we can assure it never happens again.

In the aftermath of the bombing, our citizens responded with an extraordinary outpouring of generosity, volunteering hours and financial support. Everyone knows about this now, and we are justly proud of our response. We've heard we set a new "Oklahoma standard" of caring.

But maybe not everyone knows that for a long time we could not easily escape the gloomy and confusing days of aftershock. Our downtown rebuilding plan did promise to boost our spirits and our skyline, but those were just buildings.

We lost 168 lives and could not make sense of it. We attended funerals and memorial services. We read about long, sometimes contentious days of planning a meaningful memorial site. We watched trials, sentencing hearings and finally, an execution. And still we could not fully make sense of it.

We saw many of our city's institutions struggle financially as we tried to make up for the losses of so many. We were charitable and hardworking, but we were continuously struck numb by the need for more dollars, more counseling, more time. For a long time, we lived under a shroud of sorrow, beneath a sky filled with ashes, in a city with many questions and few answers.

It seemed we might be destined to live this way forever, in a bombed-out city with holes in its heart focused on a culture of tragedy. But now after a full decade, we have set out on a new course and while it may seem abstract, it is not. We are answering our own questions and taking hold of our destiny. By surviving, rebuilding and looking forward, we are making our stand. Now we begin to understand.

This memorial — now officially called the Oklahoma City National Memorial and Museum — stands as a bastion against hatred and violence.

Last week's 10th anniversary events launched a new chapter in this unfinished story. The leadership of the Oklahoma City National Memorial made much use of the word "hope" — frequently, eloquently and, yes, hopefully. We looked back on a "Decade of Hope;" the anniversary activities, many celebratory, were part of the "Week of Hope" and at the end of that week, an award was given as "Reflections of Hope."

Yet hope in this instance is not just a wish or an expectation. It is not an inert state, but an active, determined one. It is not a passive mood that comes over us, but rather a way to act against injustice, oppression and death.

It is seen in the courageous examples of two women from Afghanistan who began an underground radio station, unheard of under the Taliban and still unimaginable in a country where women were enslaved and enshrouded. Voice of Afghan Women Radio is broadcasting information about education, employment and health; their brand of hope is daring action. If two women in war-torn Afghanistan can act against cruelty, then we in Oklahoma can stand up when we see it, too.

Is there an alternative to violence? Can we learn it? Can we teach it? We can try, and last week when 250 high school students from across Oklahoma came together at the memorial to participate in sessions in conflict resolution based on the model established by the United Nations, we did try.

Kari Watkins, the memorial's director, said they will repeat the program often, "teaching solutions to conflict that are not violent."

We cannot assure an attack of terror never happens again. It may. It happened in lower Manhattan and happens most days in the Middle East. But only by meeting violence with resistance, hatred with tolerance, can we be a city of hope. We were meant to choose life, and here, together in Oklahoma City, we are.

Epilogue

By the spring of 2007, the Reflections of Hope Award, which includes an honorarium of $25,000, had been given three times. That year, an organization called Seeds of Peace was honored for its efforts to bring teenagers together from conflict regions in the world to learn the skills of peacemaking. Begun in 1993, the international group focuses primarily on the Middle East but has expanded to programs in South Asia, Cyprus and the Balkans and now claims 3,500 young participants, including, most recently, American teens.

In 2006, the award was given to Durga Ghimire, co-founder of the Tamakoshi Service Society in Nepal for her work in guerilla-controlled areas of Ramechhap. With her husband, Jagdish, this volunteer grassroots organization has recruited more than 6,000 members in 40 villages who provide basic services in health care, agriculture and income generation.

The money that formed the initial endowment fund for the Reflections of Hope Award was provided by the Donald W. Reynolds Foundation in honor of city leader Linda Lambert for her service to the National Memorial Foundation. Lambert's concept and that of the Reynolds Foundation and the international award selection committee is to increase the size of the prize money and to gain greater recognition for the honorees and their work.

Now, four years into an American-led war in Iraq, new fighting among Palestinian factions and between them and Israel, unrest in Pakistan, hostility coming from Iran, confusion and killings in Lebanon, genocide in the Darfur region of Sudan — just to start with one region of the world — peace has never seemed so impossible. We're left with hope and a commitment to seed peace and raise peacemakers wherever and whenever we can.

A SEAL FOR ALL OF US
OCTOBER 1995

PROLOGUE

The Christian cross formerly occupied one quadrant of the official seal of Edmond, Okla., a suburban city to the north of Oklahoma City. After a three-member panel of the U.S. Court of Appeals for the 10th Judicial Circuit determined that the cross was an endorsement of religion by the city and should be removed, the city of Edmond did that, leaving the quadrant blank. The city then appealed this decision to the U.S. Supreme Court in 1996, but the Court declined to hear the case, letting the decision of the lower court stand.

he religious significance and meaning of the Latin or Christian cross are unmistakable," said a panel of three federal appeals court judges last week, deciding unanimously that the seal of the city of Edmond, Okla., violated the U.S. Constitution and advanced a particular religion.

The decision stunned many Edmond residents: "It's a bunch of hooey!" cried one for whom Christianity is a fact of life. For them, the members of this majority religion, there was no problem. On Sundays all the churches are full, said one fellow. But for those of us for whom Christianity is not a fact of our lives, the seal was an uncomfortable reminder that, in fact, we are not part of the official community.

Of course the cross is a religious symbol. Everyone with two eyes — including the Islamic, Hindu, Jewish, Buddhist and other varied citizens of Edmond — knows it to be the strongest, clearest symbol of Christianity. Besides, there are lots of reminders.

Every time I open a letter from the City of Oklahoma City, I find myself asking, "Is this my city, too?" (The invitation to the Christian Businessman's Prayer Breakfast really throws me, since I'm neither of those things.)

By the looks of the city's official letterhead, police cars, insignias on uniforms or pin given to me for service on a city commission, Oklahoma City is a Christian city. The cross on our city's seal, as sure as the cross on the official seals of Edmond, The Village and apparently many other towns in the state, says so. There never has been any pretense about it.

I didn't find the court's decision "preposterous," then, as Edmond's Mayor Bob Rudkin did. Edmond's official emblem bearing the cross is an announcement for all the world that Edmond is a religious community, specifically a Christian religious community. No pretense. No fooling anybody. No bones about it.

A little myopic maybe ("Since most of us are Christians, shouldn't our seal reflect that?"). A little insensitive, possibly ("We've always treated everyone fairly here; even if they're not Christian, they'll understand").

What would Mr. Rudkin and Edmond's council members think of a six-pointed Jewish Star of David or an Islamic crescent on their seal, their police cars, their stationery, their uniforms? Some years ago, when Muslim members of the Edmond community wanted to build a mosque there alongside Christian churches, a great uproar ensued. The mosque was eventually built, but the Muslims in Edmond were certainly reminded that their town was dominated by a Christian majority.

It could be argued that defending this symbol on the seal was a little foolhardy, too. The legal precedent for this decision was so strong, it's hard for Edmond's leaders to justify the $74,000 they spent in taxpayer money to hire an outside attorney to fight this case. A friend, not coincidentally a resident of Edmond, points out that for the approximately 61,000 residents of that town, the lawyer's bill cost each and every one of them more than $1 — Christian and non-Christian alike.

Surely they will not waste any more of their citizens' money trying to convince the U.S. Supreme Court to hear a case like several others it has already turned down.

Mr. Rudkin finds this decision preposterous. He feels there's "a concerted effort to remove all semblance of religion from public life."

There's not. There's just a concerted, time-honored, revolution-tested, constitutionally guaranteed right to remove one group's religion from official public life over any one else's. I hope Oklahoma City will follow the wisdom of the 10th judicial circuit and remove the cross from our seal, too.

Many of us who live, work, study, do business, volunteer and contribute to this city are not Christians. We do these things not because we're Christians or Jews or belong to any particular religion, but because we're neighbors. Without a cross on the seal, the neighborhood would include us all — officially.

EPILOGUE

As of February 2001, the City of Edmond had removed its original seal from most places it had appeared. The seal still appears on the flag at City Hall and depicts several other images — a landmark building on a college campus, a wagon from the days of the Oklahoma Land Run, some oil rigs and one blank, white space. The drawing of the cross never has been replaced with anything, and city attorneys tell me the old seal is no longer in use. I guess if Edmond can't say publicly that it's Christian, it won't say anything at all.

MAYOR, MAY I?

MARCH 2004

PROLOGUE

The Oklahoma City mayoral race to succeed Kirk Humphreys in the spring of 2004 was hotly contested. The two strongest candidates were Mick Cornett, a former Oklahoma City Council Member from Ward One and a radio and TV sportscaster, and Jim Tolbert, a businessman, philanthropist and civic leader.

Cornett was a Republican, Tolbert a Democrat, but the mayoral race had never been a partisan one. Candidates filed and ran without party affiliation, people voted in one election and the highest vote getter, presuming a majority, won.

Cornett won with 57 percent of the vote to Tolbert's 30 percent and lesser-known Marcus Hayes came in third.

Cornett owed his victory to his smooth, skillful campaign, the voters' familiarity with him as a sportscaster and his decision to run aggressively as a Republican against a Democrat. Cornett was aided by U.S. Rep. Ernest Istook, R-Warr Acres, who made recorded phone calls on Cornett's behalf reminding people of his conservative, Republican, Christian values and suggesting that Tolbert was a "liberal, Clinton-supporting Democrat" whose values were not what was needed to represent Oklahoma City.

(At this point, a disclosure from me is in order: "American Woman" is published by Full Circle Press, a publishing company owned by Tolbert.)

ear Mr. Mayor:

Advice, as you may know, is worth what you pay for it. But now that you're mayor, your actions are fair game for pundits like me.

Let me confess my bias up front: I supported one of your opponents.

Nevertheless, I congratulate you on your victory and genuinely wish you well. I watched the mayoral race pretty closely and have been involved in city government as well. I respectfully offer a few suggestions for mending fences, building allies and making progress for the city.

1. Any mayor, especially a new one, needs all the help he can get. In spite of your previous and laudable service to Ward One, no one expects you to have all the answers for the entire city, so don't be afraid to ask for help. There are a lot of people in town who not only can help you; they will want to help you.

Start with a call to Cliff Hudson, the Oklahoma City Public Schools board president. All four candidates for mayor, including you, rightly said fully finishing MAPS for Kids is the most significant piece of business for Oklahoma City. You and Hudson will need to work closely together, communicating openly and honestly. The strong partnership established between the city and the school board during former mayor Kirk Humphreys' terms needs to remain strong.

You might also benefit from the aid of former opponents Jim Tolbert and Marcus Hayes. Tolbert, for his sage wisdom and decades of work for the city, was a formidable opponent. There has hardly been a city commission or committee on which he has not served. He knows a lot, is gracious about helping, and would likely welcome any call from you. Think about the best way to put him back to work, and I am betting he will be glad to help.

Hayes is a new and promising talent. He is frighteningly young, 27, but has a strong combination of traits to offer. He is passionate about public service; he is compassionate about the less advantaged in the city. He is appealing, articulate and, as a black, represents a constituency whose contributions we cannot do without.

Reach out; invite them in. Enlarge your tent.

2. You are good with the media – good on television and radio, good at communicating your ideas and smart about what the print and broadcast media need from public figures. You know, too, what a powerful tool press attention can be. Use these skills to sell your initiatives, convey your enthusiasm, and build a bigger, better-educated forum for city issues.

Neither the Daily Oklahoman nor most local television stations gave enough coverage to this mayoral race. The Oklahoman even made the curious decision not to run stories about the race in its front section, relegating news of candidates and the campaign to short, hidden stories and then only in the Metro section. I can't see how that's helping to build an informed electorate.

Television and radio really are your business. Perhaps television news directors could be convinced to give more airtime to municipal issues. Both the Gazette, KFOR Channel 4, KTOK-AM 1000 and WKY-AM 930 radio stations gave significant coverage to this race. Keep them in the game by offering interviews, stories and background.

3. The Oklahoma City mayor's office is not a partisan one. When they run your name under your picture on television or in the newspaper, they will not say "Mayor Mick Cornett, Republican." They will not say, "Conservative Mayor Cornett." You have every right to be, vote and associate with Republicans, Democrats, independents, Tories or Whigs. But as Mayor of Oklahoma City, you are mayor, and your political affiliations don't count. In that way, you are on your own.

The partisan polarization going on in this country, in this state and now, in this city, is worse than at any time I can remember. That's only good news for political consultants and those who would use you and your position as mayor to promote their own party. It's bad news for the rest of us.

Most of us don't know – or care – which political party our city council representatives or mayor belong to. There's been as much good, and as much harm, done for this city by Republicans as Democrats. Call yourself conservative or liberal or even a Yankees fan, but leave the labels outside the door to City Hall. Go to work for all of us.

E P I L O G U E

In 2005, just a few months after his election as mayor, Cornett ran for the Republican nomination to fill the U.S. House seat of retiring House member Istook. The district was gerrymandered for the Republicans by the state Legislature in 2004, and it was almost a fait accompli that the Republicans would keep the seat. The primary was crowded with five strong candidates.

There was some unhappiness with Cornett for holding his place as mayor while running for Congress, and the state Legislature briefly considered a measure to make such a thing illegal.

Cornett and Mary Fallin, Oklahoma's former lieutenant governor, made it through the primary into a runoff election that Fallin won with 63 percent of the vote. In the general election, Fallin defeated Democrat David Hunter and won the congressional seat handily.

Cornett went back to City Hall and was re-elected to a second term on March 7, 2007, by an 87.6 percent margin, the largest in Oklahoma City history.

JARI IN THE HOUSE

APRIL 2004

J ari Askins, a four-term state representative from Duncan, Okla., could become the first woman in the state's history to rise to the powerful position of speaker of the Oklahoma House of Representatives. All eyes are on Askins, and her fellow Democrats, as she guides the 2004 election season, poised to lead the 2005 state Legislature.

Askins will assume this key post if, and only if, Democrats hold onto their slim majority in the state House in November's elections. If not — if Republicans win over a few seats to claim the majority — we will have lost the chance for Askins to lead the House and bring, for the first time, a woman's point of view to legislative leadership in the state.

The 53-to-48 Democrat majority is threatened largely by the political havoc created by term limits. Eighteen of those 53 Democrat members will see their terms expire at the end of this legislative session, and four others are seeking different office. That means voters will have to elect 22 Democrats to refill those seats. Candidate recruitment and fund-raising for these seats began at least a year ago with Askins at the helm and with the help of current Speaker Larry Adair, D-Stillwell. But this numbers game is tough.

The Republicans will have a lot of money from state and national sources, But both parties predict tight races, and the Republicans may get a ride on W's coattails.

Will it make a difference having a woman in charge? Many studies and many people instinctively say "yes." Were it not for women in legislative bodies and Congress, little if any attention would have been paid to family medical leave policies, reproductive freedom issues, pay

36

equity, more parity in insurance coverage, and the inclusion of women in many aspects of health research.

There are a handful of women legislative leaders across the country, but since Oklahoma ranks very low in the number of women elected to those bodies, having a woman leader may not do much to increase numbers. Still, electing a woman to a leadership role is important.

Askins, an attorney, was a judge in Stephens County and formerly chaired the state's Pardon and Parole Board. Her experience is probably deepest in criminal justice and on behalf of "special victims" — children and victims of domestic assault — and in criminal justice reform.

She never takes on an issue unless she knows it well, said Jay Parmley, state Democrat Party chair. And, he added, she has the respect of her colleagues because she is a workhorse on all issues.

Askins' strength seems to be in her character, her experience, and her decent and levelheaded approach to lawmaking. Known for operating with integrity, she appears to have little patience for political manipulation, but she certainly understands practical politics. Her longtime friend and fellow Duncanite State Treasurer Robert Butkin, said, "Jari raises the quality of public debate; she's always a voice of reason."

Janet Wilson, a University of Oklahoma faculty member and champion against domestic violence said, "Jari negotiates with the ol' boy crowd. And she seems to have fun doing it!"

As speaker-designate, Askins gives the party an opportunity to register, motivate and turn out women voters, new voters, and possibly crossover voters looking for a different approach to lawmaking.

Should the Democrats lose the majority in the state House, it will make an already obstreperous, nastily bipartisan, increasingly conservative Oklahoma political landscape more of all of that. The Democrat governor will have his enemies in his face, and the Democrat state Senate and House could be at constant loggerheads.

But the real defeat will be the lost opportunity to have Askins show us how it can be done. A vote for your Democrat lawmaker this fall is not just a vote for politics as usual; it's a vote for a new kind of leadership, Jari Askins, a woman to run our House.

EPILOGUE

In the 2004 Oklahoma elections, the Democrats lost their majority in the state House of Representatives, handing it over to the Republicans for the first time in decades and leaving Askins to settle for minority leader.

Wanting a bigger leadership role, Askins ran statewide for lieutenant governor and was elected in 2006. In this job, she serves as president of the state Senate and on numerous boards and commissions. She chairs the Oklahoma Tourism and Recreation Commission, the Oklahoma Film and Music Advisory Commission, and Gov. Brad Henry named her Oklahoma's Small Business Advocate.

It's not a powerful post, but it is a visible one. And it got Askins out of the stymied House where frustration is often the prevailing mood.

Since the Democrats lost the majority in the state House and nearly lost the state Senate, Henry, a Democrat, has had a rough time "leading" the Legislature toward his budget and his programs, even as he enjoys great popularity among voters. Divided government certainly makes for a diversity of opinions, but not for moving along the already-slow wheels of lawmaking.

As for Askins, her move to the executive branch can only help her if she chooses to seek higher office. I'm hoping she will.

THE WORD ON OKLAHOMA
NOVEMBER 2002

he word on Oklahoma is conservative.

Conservative about government. Conservative economically. Conservative about social issues. Conservative — for sure! — about politics.

Ask people outside Oklahoma to describe our state's political leanings and that's what you hear, from the press, to pundits, to pollsters, to politicians, to plain ol' people. Oklahoma really has become conservative, they say, wondering what happened to the approach of moderate Oklahoma icons like Henry Bellmon and David Boren, good-humored populists like Fred Harris and Will Rogers, and even populist liberals like former Congressmen Jim Jones and Mike Synar. Now we're described as very conservative. Ultra-conservative. Right-wing conservative.

Conservative was certainly the favored word used by Republican candidates to describe themselves in this last election. They ran on "Oklahoma's conservative values," or "conservative Christian values" or "conservative family values." I had begun to think the strong tradition of populism, the preference for moderation, and the openness of the frontier-style big tent that once marked Oklahoma's spirit had gone.

But Brad Henry's upset victory over Steve Largent for the top job in our state may have proved me and other observers of the state wrong.

One of the candidates most proud to declare himself conservative in this last election was Largent, once considered a shoo-in for governor. Largent, an attractive young Republican congressman and former professional football player from Tulsa, let it be known early he was interested in being governor. Republicans inside and outside the state were delighted. He fit the profile and the mold. Nice guy, handsome, great athlete and conservative. Very conservative. This time last year, the race was Largent's to lose.

But Oklahomans didn't buy Largent. While he proudly painted himself as conservative — and has the public record to prove it — Henry let Largent's record speak for itself and Oklahomans rejected it. Largent doesn't just espouse his conservative philosophy; he goes way beyond, harshly judging any others' views as wrong, just wrong.

For example, Largent doesn't just oppose keeping abortion legal and safe or including gays in civil rights legislation; he sees both unrelated issues as "unhealthy lifestyle choices" and is proud to say so. He suggested a Catholic priest might be divisive as a chaplain in Congress, angrily embroiling himself in a national controversy from which he would not back down.

Largent doesn't operate by compromising and building consensus, and it showed. In Congress, he ran for House Majority Leader in 1998, challenging Dick Armey, who won 127–95. After his defeat Largent testily said, "I'm not accustomed to losing. I don't like to lose."

In his campaign for governor, Largent's too stubborn, too flinty, too pompous brand of conservatism didn't translate for Oklahoma voters either. He made little effort to discuss or honestly debate his philosophy. He seemed to be saying, "I'm a conservative, you get it and that's enough." In other words, my way or the highway.

His now-infamous *faux pas* occurred in a televised debate. Largent, irritated by a comment, characteristically lost his cool and spat out "bull shit!" He later apologized, but the damage was done. It wasn't the cussing that nettled people — who hasn't used those words in annoyance? It was his intemperance and his inability to show restraint in a public forum that didn't ring true with the conservative label he had chosen for himself.

Extremists of any philosophy — ultra conservative or ultra liberal — often come off as arrogant, believing in the unquestionable rightness of their views and dismissing everyone else's. Henry is no liberal, nor was that the contrast between him and Largent. Rather than a choice between an extreme conservative and an extreme liberal, voters perceived, I think, a choice between an arrogant, die-hard conservative and a deferential, uncomplicated moderate.

When I moved to Oklahoma in the early Eighties, I found the state's leaders to be an interesting mix of Democrats, Republicans and independents, moderates, liberals and conservatives. The congressional delegation boasted moderate U.S. Senators Bellmon and Boren. Moderate-conservatives Glen English, a Democrat, and Mickey Edwards, a Republican, were in the House with centrist-moderate Democrats Dave McCurdy and Wes Watkins. Jones and Synar were liberal-leaning moderates. Democrats may have controlled the state Legislature, but extremists there, such as liberal Cleta Deatherage Mitchell and extreme conservative John Monks stuck out like sore thumbs. I was impressed by an absence of polarizing labels.

But the mid-Nineties saw the election of much more conservative politicians: Sens. Jim Inhofe, R-Tulsa, and Don Nickles, R-Ponca City; and U.S. Reps. Ernest Istook, R-Oklahoma City, Tom Coburn, R-Muskogee, J.C. Watts, R-Norman, and Largent. With the 2002 election the pendulum has begun to swing back a little toward center.

Even newly elected Congressman Tom Cole, R-Norman, kingmaker of many Republicans and a man comfortable with the conservative label, isn't really a conservative ideologue. He may ascribe to conservative political philosophies, but not extremely so. And he presents himself as affable and respectful. Mostly, Cole's a strategist, but even he had a tough race.

Extremists can't govern. They can run, they can make a lot of racket, and they can raise a lot of money, but they don't usually govern well. Compliance and compromise, measure and moderation, are important assets for office holders trying to help solve a state's problem. Oklahomans — independent-minded people who don't like fanatic approaches to anything save religion – bet in this election on moderation. By electing Henry, and re-electing most of the top office holders in the state, the word on Oklahoma is, once again, moderate.

Epilogue

Henry did beat Largent. He has been an extremely popular governor in Oklahoma, launching a statewide lottery to fund education, supporting teacher salary increases, and working to pass a cigarette tax to fund health care, among other things. A folksy style, a non-partisan and cautious approach to politics, Henry drew notable, but not serious opposition in 2006 in his bid for re-election from former U.S. Rep. Ernest Istook, R-Oklahoma City. He easily defeated Istook with 66 percent of the vote, a higher vote than any gubernatorial candidate in Oklahoma has received in 50 years.

Honest, plain speaking and always appearing with a beautiful, intelligent wife and three loveable daughters, Henry must leave the statehouse in 2008. Henry's popularity is solid – as long as he it plays it down the middle, his preference anyway. And he could be a strong, moderate candidate against bizarre, fanatic U.S. Sen. Tom Coburn, R-Muskogee.

After Largent's defeat, the former football player, then congressman, then losing gubernatorial candidate, did what many "former members" of Congress do: He took up permanent residence in Washington, D.C., and become a lobbyist.

Is the word on Oklahoma still conservative? Yes, and no.

In the 2004 national elections, George W. Bush carried all 77 counties in Oklahoma, making Oklahoma one of the "reddest of the red" states. In state politics, however, "there is vigorous two-party competition and Democrats still have an edge in party registration. But they are conservative Democrats," wrote Mike Barone in his 2006 Almanac of American Politics.

Oklahoma still sends one of the most conservative and one of the most Bush-supporting delegations in the country to Washington, even as Bush's approval ratings dip to record-breaking lows. Based on the 2000 census, Oklahoma lost a seat in Congress, so as of this writing, Oklahoma has only five members of Congress (four very conservative Republicans and one conservative Democrat.) We have also elected two exceptionally conservative U.S. Senators to the capitol – Inhofe and Coburn – and it is through them that much of the country gets its official impression of us.

A GESTURE OF RESPECT

MAY 1990

I once lived in a big, crowded city where you only stopped your car for red lights and, in some neighborhoods, not even then. Getting where I had to go, on my time and my terms, was all that mattered once I slid behind the wheel of my car and bowed my neck for the self-absorbed journey across town going about my own business.

Occasionally, in the noisy chaos of the city, you'd see a hearse and some headlit cars in funeral procession. If it even occurred to you to stop, you'd dismiss it as unnecessary, unimportant and definitely unsafe. There was no police escort, certainly not a vital use of scarce city funds. So you'd grumble, "Someone's funeral," and impatiently look for a way to dart around the procession, lest you be delayed even two more minutes.

But people in Oklahoma stop their cars when a funeral procession passes. It was one of the first things I noticed here. There was time and space, and police help, to interrupt your own journey and acknowledge someone else's.

We have all been, or will be, in one of those cars in one of those processions. Moving through traffic beside friends and relatives who share your sadness, you look out of the shaded car window and watch life go on around you.

"Look at them," you find yourself thinking.

"To them, this is just a normal street, a normal route on their way to a normal, everyday kind of task. But for us in this car, on this street, this whole world seems to have stopped.

"Today our route is different from what it's ever been before. Can't they see that? How can everyone go on about his business when the business of our lives has stopped, nothing short of dead in its tracks?

"How can others go to restaurants for chatty, casual lunches when we are filing into the funeral home? How can they carry briefcases and grocery bags while we are carrying a casket? Is this loss ours alone? Are we so uniquely struck by this sorrow that our lives are the only lives called to a halt today?"

The business of living life does and should go on around, before, during and after a death. Nor do we expect or even want total strangers intimately involved in our grief.

But it is remarkably comforting to drive past delivery trucks, station wagons, pickups and sports cars, all of whose drivers have pulled over and stopped, managing to put a halt, too, to their busy lives just long enough to acknowledge some connection to our sadness and say, "We all know, or will eventually, just how you must feel."

THREE

FAMILY MATTERS

LOSING BUNNY
MAY 1996

sparkling, sunny spring weekend in the East, the snow had finally melted, and we were en route to a family weekend at our son's college. We piled our baggage and ourselves into a rental car at Boston's big, chaotic Logan Airport and headed south.

As we left the parking lot, our 12-year-old daughter cried out from the back seat.

"Oh, no," she moaned. "I left Bunny on the plane."

Bunny. A stuffed white rabbit more gray now than white, more unstuffed than stuffed.

Bunny. Last seen with pink ears wearing white cotton undies. The underpants weren't originally Bunny's, but he — or she; none of us has known for sure about Bunny's sexual orientation nor cared — was embarrassed by a bare behind, so Bunny was always properly covered with some borrowed skivvies.

Bunny. Who slept with her, snuggled with her, comforted and loved her and went everywhere with her since she was a toddler. Bunny. Now missing, probably gone. Fighting back tears, she struggled mightily to cope with what was for her a significant loss.

The next day would be her 13th birthday.

The next week she would begin to view her parents — the same parents who had always been her consolation, her support, her heroes — with annoyance, impatience and disdain for their astounding stupidity.

The next month she would become a Bat Mitzvah, meaning a "daughter and keeper of the commandments" in a Jewish coming-of-age ceremony. Beginning with this ritual, she is expected and privileged to accept the adult responsibilities of her family's faith and community.

She looked at me soulfully, with the sad, wide blue eyes of my baby and the strong, wiser eyes of my soon-to-be young woman. I saw both of her sitting there in the back of the car, seat belt securely fastened.

Bunny was gone. The transition from childhood to womanhood had officially begun.

While boys have become Bar Mitzvah ("Sons of the commandment") since the sixth century C.E., the ceremony was not held for girls until 1922 when a rabbi introduced it to his congregation in New York for his own daughter. Now girls, too, are called before their congregations to participate in the Sabbath service and read from the Torah, the first five books of Moses. At last, a girl's transition from childhood to womanhood is honored in Judaism, too.

This girl has approached this occasion as she does most things, with determination, focus and street-smart good sense. She has found the daunting task of learning the language, values and rituals of her ancestors interesting. She has managed the typical teenager's balancing act — schoolwork, Hebrew school, daily pre-dawn training as a competitive figure skater, softball and, of course, a "heavy social life" — as a cheerful challenge.

It's hard work, but the harder the work, the better she likes it. Childhood and girlhood have been pretty smooth sailing for this girl.

But now, things could get more complicated. Soon she will begin choosing and preparing for her own life's work. Soon her street smarts will be tested, on and off the streets.

Almost as if to signal her entrance to young adulthood, Bunny disappeared. And with him innocence, simplicity and perfect love.

Bunny, asking for nothing, giving everything.

Bunny and his perfect love will be replaced with real love. This is how life works. Soon, there will be other loves and other losses — a friend, a boy, a man, a family. All most difficult, some more painful. No one can give or get perfect love.

" 'Real isn't how you are made,' " said the Skin Horse to the rabbit in the Margery Williams children's classic, "The Velveteen Rabbit."

"'It's a thing that happens to you. When a child loves you for a long, long, time, not just to play with, but REALLY loves you, then you become Real.'"

"'Does it hurt?'" asked the Rabbit."

"'Sometimes,'" said the Skin Horse, "for he was always truthful."

"'When you are Real you don't mind being hurt … It doesn't happen all at once … It takes a long time … once you are Real, you can't become unreal again. It lasts for always.'"

Welcome to womanhood, my girl. Expect its losses, rejoice in its love.

IRONMAN
OCTOBER 1987

At first I thought it was just bananas. The yellow kind. Without realizing it, I was buying dozens each week.

Then odd things began showing up in the pantry: boxes of a non-narcotic white powder, green and foul-tasting when mixed with water and subtly called Exceed. Next appeared hundreds of revolting whole-grain products, such as PowerBars, a form of flavored, compressed cardboard loaded with energy-inducers. And finally, in the garage, an Italian bicycle with French chains and a wheel without spokes.

What was going on?

My husband finally confessed — naturally after the plans were a *fait accompli* — he had submitted his name for entry in the Ironman contest, the ultimate triathlon held each year in Kona, Hawaii. This endurance test requires a 2.4-mile ocean swim (yes, sharks have been spotted), a 112-mile bike ride and a 26.2-mile marathon run. And wouldn't you know it, they chose his name. Out of a jar. Some people have all the luck.

"You actually want to do this?" I asked incredulously.

"Oh, God!" worried his parents. "He's so thin!"

To describe this man as obsessive is to state the obvious. To describe me as frazzled and fragmented is also a given. All I know about working out is aerobic eating.

So you really had to be there to appreciate the negotiations over his six-month, five-hours-a-day training schedule. There was a lot of, "When this is over … " and "Next year it's your turn, dear." After kicking and screaming (this technique does not work on obsessive types), I gave up and said, "Go and be well."

So off he went, biking, running and swimming all over this state and a few others to prepare for the ordeal. Some days he'd leave home on his bike at 6 a.m., returning late that afternoon from trekking to nearby towns like Luther, Okla., where his chief excitement was a chase from a stray pig or an admiring truck driver. He lived on Exceed, shredded wheat and determination. I lived on blind faith and diminishing patience and counted the days.

A week before the race, he left early for Hawaii to get used to the water and the terrain. Despite rumors, he did not swim over.

A week later, I arrived with our two kids, ages 10 and four, the day before the race. Immediately, we were swept up in the melee of 1,500 super-athletes and 4,000 awe-struck spectators watching and waiting.

Race day. 7 a.m. Into the Pacific waters they dove, bathed in the spectacularly beautiful sunrise over the Kona Coast, inspired by a display of Hawaiian hoopla and thrilled to be part of this exciting, nationally televised, world-class athletic event.

At each transition point, we caught a glimpse of our Ironman and cheered him on to the next event.

He raced out of the water and into his bike shoes and was off again. We three fans returned to the hotel, lunched, swam, napped and downed a few piña coladas in his honor. Six hours later, our triathlete tossed his bike and began the run, at 2:30 p.m. in the 90-degree-plus heat.

And then, way past sundown and 11 hours and 43 minutes after he began, he crossed the finish line.

To see it was to understand only part of the fantastic accomplishment it was. He beat his own "personal best." He finished in the top 35 percent, and even higher in his age group. His pride and happiness were mirrored by ours.

Finishing strong was a great feat, but the training was much of the accomplishment. Since May, he had biked more than 2,700 miles, run 650 miles and swam 218,000 yards.

An hour after the race, he wolfed down a cheeseburger, french fries, a Coke and apple pie. That might have been the best news of the day.

Congratulations and welcome back, Ironman.

GAS OUT OF GRASS

SEPTEMBER 2006

live with a man who wants to make gas out of grass.

I live with a man who talks to himself and anyone who will listen about farmland, feedstock and fuel tanks. I live with a man who has spent most of his adult life trying to figure out where and how to get oil and natural gas out of the ground.

Now he wants to use much of that ground to plant a bunch of grass and weedy-lookin' stuff to grow our state's economy, cut greenhouse emissions, and help our nation become more secure.

I thought we were past some of my husband's long-abiding obsessions. There were years of marathons and long-distance cycling and winter seasons of packing his skis, unwavering in his promise to himself to get in those "20 days of skiing every year."

Single-minded in his determination to ace each of these tests, each hurdle has been Him vs. Something Else Bigger Than Him. (At this point, I should reveal that "him" is my husband, David Fleischaker, the Governor's Secretary of Energy and an independent oil and gas producer of many years, hereinafter, a.k.a. David.)

It's been David vs. the bike track, David vs. the black diamond slopes, David vs. the rocks at the Washita National Wildlife Refuge. Now it's David attacking, in his public servant role, the undeniable problem that we, as a state, nation and world, are in big trouble, having relied for too long and too heavily on a gradually diminishing supply of carbon fuels (oil and natural gas) to feed the fires of our manufacturing, transportation, defense, agriculture, automotive and virtually every other industry in America.

David (I refuse to call him Mr. Secretary) is not suggesting the oil and gas industry in Oklahoma should be replaced. We will need, he says, energy from every source possible, and petroleum production will always be a mainstay in Oklahoma.

But now he is convinced that by planting certain hearty, drought-resistant, perennial prairie grasses all over the plains of Oklahoma, our farmers and ranchers can ultimately produce an essential, clean, renewable and alternative source of energy, complementing our diminishing supply of oil and gas. Biofuels-as-an-energy-source has already been seeded in the minds and plans of some important players. The Noble Foundation in Ardmore, Okla., is committed to developing these plant sources; both the University of Oklahoma and Oklahoma State University have programs to research these crops; some major oil and gas companies have dedicated time and money in the pursuit of prairie grasses as alternative fuel sources; the federal government is handing out some money to explore it; and Oklahoma's farmers, ranchers, conservationists and environmentalists are finding ways to join together to make this idea work for them in Oklahoma.

"GROW: Oklahoma Governor's Conference on Biofuels" will bring together some of the nation's most important doers and thinkers on biofuels Oct. 3-4, 2006, at the student union on the OU campus. The keynote speaker, James Woolsey, former director of the CIA, will hammer home the security dangers in continued reliance on foreign oil for our transportation needs. Speakers from private industry, the government and universities will talk about their commitment to developing biofuels. The details are at www.growOK.com.

Planting and refining switchgrass into fuel may not be as much fun as planning your next ski trip. But it's worth it for Oklahoma's future — and a better obsession for the man I live with than hang gliding, something new he muttered about in his sleep last night.

Epilogue

The "GROW" Conference of 2006 was a big success, with 650 attendees from 18 states ranging in interest from government laboratory and university researchers, industry executives, professional investors, federal and state government officials and most importantly, farmers and ranchers interested in learning more about dedicated energy crops. A second conference planned for the fall of 2007 promises to expand on the first.

Since Gov. Brad Henry appointed my husband to be his cabinet Secretary of Energy in 2003, developing alternatives to carbon-based energy sources has become one of the most pressing issues in the public's mind and the government's as well. In President Bush's 2006 State of the Union address, the former Texas oilman surprised people by saying, "We are addicted to oil."

Energy policy wonks, like David, already knew this, and have helped launch a rapidly growing movement to find, develop and make viable a growing industry in biofuels, geothermal generation, wind power, etc. It is a matter of national security and a matter of environmental necessity.

Here in Oklahoma, the 2007 state Legislature approved $10 million to fund the Oklahoma Bioenergy Center, a collaboration between OU, OSU and the Noble Foundation to develop a biofuels industry in the state, with an additional $10 million hoped for over three more years.

My husband has thrown himself into alternative energy development much like he did marathons and skiing.

And so far, we've avoided hang gliding. But did I mention yoga? He's taken up yoga. Not the calm, meditative, relaxing yoga for him, though. It's power yoga, of course. Maybe he could persuade the Legislature to change his title to the Secretary With Energy. Namaste.

THE WHOLE CHILD
AUGUST 1996

t takes three alarm clocks, at least one parent — rapidly aging, I might add — and remarkable motivation for my 13-year-old daughter to drag herself out of bed at 4 a.m., five days a week.

She pulls on two pairs of warm-up tights, a skimpy practice dress, a sweatshirt and wool gloves. She eats, loads water, snacks and stiff, expensive skates with sharp, expensive blades into a heavy bag and flies out the door in the dark to be driven to a skating rink way across town.

She skates two hours on weekday mornings before school and five hours on summer mornings. She competes three or four times a year in different cities. She's usually tired and sore. Some days are great: "I skated two clean programs during practice!" Some aren't: "I'll never get my double lutz, and I may kill myself trying." But she loves it, loves the hard work, the friendships, her coach, the music, the costumes. Most of all, she loves the satisfaction that comes from doing something difficult and doing it well.

The 1996 women's Olympic gymnastics competition and the accompanying publicity about injuries, young competitors, emotional and physical trauma and coaches who act like monsters was enough to give the parent of any athlete anxiety.

Watching American gymnast Kerri Strug fall, hurt herself badly, then get up and do it again all for "The Gold," was nearly unbearable. Yes, she was a brave little girl. But mostly, she is a little girl.

She would probably say she loves her sport, too. But do we see joy for the sport on these girls' faces, or everyone else's expectations — parents', coaches', friends'? How can a 13-year-old know what she wants from life or how much to sacrifice to get it?

Three doctors writing in the New England Journal of Medicine landed hard on organized gymnastics for the hardships it imposes on young girls. They list an alarming array of common physical injuries — stress fractures, delayed puberty, scoliosis, higher risk of osteoporosis and arthritis — and warn against emotional damage, as well. They find 62 percent of elite gymnasts have eating disorders, and depression is rampant among these girls who peak at 14, 15 or 16 and are left with damaged bodies, damaged psyches and little youth.

In a book, "Little Girls in Pretty Boxes: The Making and Breaking of Elite Gymnasts and Figure Skaters," the stories are even worse, portraying parents and their daughters as pawns in the hands of egomaniacal coaches. The book tells of anorexic girls, girls living and training in constant pain, and suicidal girls.

So what to do about all this? Close down ice rinks that are springing up across the country to support this growing and popular sport? Return leotards and skates from thousands of little ones who start out having fun in gym class but may end up with shattered bodies and lives? Should we fire all the coaches?

None of this is possible or necessary. Not every gymnast or figure skater will get an elite ranking or go to the Olympics. But each of them can learn and grow and enjoy the unbeatable feeling of self-worth that comes from focusing energy and discipline on hard work without destroying body and soul in the process.

Another book about young girls, "Raising Ophelia," reports a different point of view. Girls involved in sports, it says, often find it easier to stay away from drugs, alcohol and tobacco. And they place much greater value on personal accomplishment than the empty status that comes from clothes or money or hanging with the "in" crowd.

The key to avoiding this obsession with making perfect athletes out of imperfect, growing children is us, their parents. Yes, the gymnastic and figure skating associations and the Olympic committees should impose rules that hold a coach's feet to the fire about training hours, injuries, competitors' ages, etc., as surely as they impose rules about how two feet must land on a mat for a "stuck" landing or how many revolutions make a medal-winning triple axel.

But parents are in charge of their children; coaches are only in charge of them as athletes. We cannot give over our children or our values to coaches or the pursuit of medals. Parents must work with coaches and athletic groups to insist on rest, nutrition, positive emotional support and encouragement for their kids. No parent or coach in their right mind should allow a child to pound on a vault horse or a cold, icy surface with a serious injury.

Training our children to be athletes is fine, but first we have to train them to respect their bodies and take care of themselves. The coach's job is to raise a child to be an athlete, respecting the whole child. A parent's job is to raise that whole child, training her to do her best to live a full, happy life – emotionally, intellectually, athletically.

TEETERING ACROSS A STAGE
MAY 1997

n that star-studded evening when I accept my award for Best Mother in a Producing/Supporting/Directing/Editing role, I will certainly thank the following who have made my job easier:

- The designers of shoes for girls who, in a desperate reading of their profit and loss statements, dreamed up 6 x 3-inch cork heels with platforms for 15-year-olds.

- Hair colorists or pop artists or whoever the hell is making it possible for children to color (read: dye, paint, crayon, spray, glitter, dip) their hair any hue of black, purple, puce or whatever.

- The piercers among you offering any number of adorable accessories for plugging the holes you've already made (and charged for) in our children. Rings and studs for the ears, eyebrows, nose, navel. Bars for the tongue not, unfortunately, restraining bars on the tongue, just unbelievably ugly and painful ways to decorate that already too-busy body part.

- All of you fashion queens campaigning to educate children about unsafe sex while designing clothing that makes every unsure-of-herself 13-year-old girl an irresistibly seductive target in navel-bearing, cleavage-foisting T-shirts and shorts.

- You clever advertising execs who market this silly stuff in magazine and TV ads for girls younger than 17.

- And last but not least, all you super-smart script writers who include story lines about teachers seducing 16-year-olds; fathers seducing daughters, and working girls comparing orgasms over expensive wines at dinner.

Thank you, thank you, all of you. Doing this job feels practically impossible most of the time, anyway. Thanks for raising the challenges while dramatically lowering the standards.

If my daughter and her pals are reading this — and because their media-savvy little brain cells are always scanning, you can be sure they are — they will no doubt roll their eyes and write me off with an annoyed, "Whatever."

But dork though I may be, I do get it. It's middle school graduation week for my daughter, a time of high excitement and high anxiety. As she looks back on 11 years in a school that has been the source of growth, security, intellectual and emotional challenges, she doesn't want to leave. Who can blame her? School will never again be so sweet and nurturing.

As the curtain opens on a new stage, high school, she may be excited and hopeful, but mostly she is scared. Scared because it isn't just her friend or her brother or the kids in her math class who will be doing this new thing, it is she — the center of attention, the one of whom there will be expectations and demands, the one who will matter the most. Even walking across the stage is scary.

How will I do it? She must be wondering. How will I stand all that focus on me, all those new and difficult things? How will I do this away from a place where I feel so safe and in a new place where I only feel — me?

"Me," of course, is the issue. She cannot know yet who she really is, but she is searching madly in every direction to find out, and the easiest place to start is on the outside. She wants to make this transition, to walk across that graduation stage looking as special and sure of herself as she knows she should be feeling. She wants special hair, a special dress, a special necklace and, naturally, special, very tall shoes, all sort-of-but-not-exactly like everyone else's. If it's too old or too tall or too risky for her, she wants them anyway. At least she will look the part, even though she may be feeling "whatever."

Every middle school mother I know this week is doing battle over platform shoes, hair color and low-cut dresses. But I think I'll stop. She will walk onto that transitional stage looking exactly like who she is; a girl becoming a young woman; a girl becoming herself in her sweet, delicate dress and clunky, tough-girl shoes.

She may not be so certain, but I am confident that all this apprehension and uncertainty teeters atop a sure and solid foundation we have all worked hard to build. Her balancing act has just begun.

Epilogue

Ten years have passed since my teen teetered across her middle school graduation stage. She's since graduated from high school wearing a cap, gown and flats, and then from college, wearing a different colored cap, gown and probably flip-flops, but I couldn't see that far.

Now a working girl in Manhattan, she's trampled through snow and sleet, rain, running paths, subway grime, taxi rides, street traffic, foot traffic and office traffic. She's run through lots of shoes, boots and flip-flops, and because she's in New York, this assortment of footwear is chic, too expensive and all must-haves. She's also running through this very exciting part of her life with full-out joy.

The late Nineties TV hit "Sex and the City" titillated and tantalized her and many of her 20-something friends. They work hard, play hard and meet in restaurants, analyzing men, life, food, men, clothes, politics, families and men, while eating and drinking and talking about every delicious detail of it.

As for the shoes, I think she wears stylish-but-sensible pumps or flats to work, but who knows. They might be five-inch platforms for all I know, and the first I'll hear about it will be a bill from a podiatrist trying to solve heel pain or bunions. But then I just gave up high heels myself last year, so don't ask me about sensible shoes. I say wear that sexy footwear 'til the last possible minute. Shoes do, indeed, make the girl.

YOU'RE FIRED!

JULY 2006

y friend called her 22-year-old daughter one day last week. Jessica, a pretty, bright, working woman in Manhattan, flipped open her cell phone and gritted her teeth.

"Mom, why are you calling?" the young woman snapped, the irritation in her voice fairly sizzling through the cell. "We just talked yesterday!"

Bucking up against her feelings of rejection, my friend knew she shouldn't take the rebuff personally and tried hard to set the minor yet stinging episode aside.

The next day, Jessica woke up with a whopper stomach virus, had to miss a day at her new job, and panicked. She called home three times with entreaties to her mom.

"What do I do? What should I take? Oh, Mom, help!"

"Oh, help!" is indeed the clarion call for this dilemma, a plea from all moms and daughters trying to sort out our once clear, now somewhat battered roles in each other's lives. "Try Tylenol, sweetie," or "Find a doctor," are acceptable answers. "I'll get on the next flight and bring chicken soup to you," is not.

Like tectonic plates under our feet, the earth on which mothers and daughters stand shifts as our girls leave the security of high school or college for the bigger, rougher Real World. And there's nothing like a feverish Graduation Weekend to reveal the cracks in this seemingly solid ground.

With great excitement, but differing expectations, The Big Weekend goes something like this:

- She's glad you're in town, but mostly wants one last (she fills in here) beer, cookout, sleepover with friends. But you want her to spend time with (Mom fills in here) her cousins, her bills, her packing, you. Guess who wins.

- She doesn't care what she wears to the graduation ceremony; she claims nobody does, so she will throw something together under the cap and gown. You wish she'd bought something attractive a week ago and had it altered, ironed and ready to go. You could get up at 8 a.m. and beg a store to open to pick up something you'd love to see her wear, but she'd probably toss it in a pile of other rejects and wear what she'd planned in the first place. Then you'll be stuck returning it.

- She's thrilled to have her friends and family mix at her apartment, come one, come all. But did she plan for this? No, Mom, that's YOUR idea. You can't believe no one has cleaned the place in anticipation and watch in horror as your aunt trips on the sticky kitchen floor.

While the ground quakes and you tug and pull at each other, moms can get their loving arms dislocated, their bank accounts mauled or even their hearts broken. And daughters can turn on a strappy, sandaled stiletto shoe and march out the door, fed up with being mothered, leaving you to wonder what went wrong and why the adorable, accomplished little ingrate doesn't see the Importance of the Occasion.

This much I know to be true: Mom, as you knew her, has been fired.

Maybe not "go-away-and-never-come-back" fired, but definitely moved to consultant status. And not a regular, predictable kind of consultant, either. Occasional suggestions are more like it, that occasion to be determined by Her.

So what's an old mom to do with these feelings of being not much use to her daughter? Of being yanked around on the ends of her directionless tethers? Of being depended upon to help with everything for years and now being told, please, do not touch that!

I thought a career would be a firewall against this feeling of loss. I thought time to relax, travel and read more books would make up for it. I thought my own mother had been silly — needy, insecure, unfulfilled — because her empty nest left her feeling, well, so empty. But of course she was neither silly nor empty. She just didn't see what she still had.

Take off the cap and gown, and my wonderful daughter is still there. If now I can stand beside her instead of in front of her, I may thrill at the road she chooses. If I button my own lip instead of the top of her too-revealing sweater, I will see her present herself to the world, her way, not mine. If I enjoy my new role as wizened consultant and quit mourning the old, tired, full-time, underpaid, grasping-in-the-dark mom, we'll both have more room to spread out and enjoy whatever comes next.

But she should read the fine print. I can't actually be fired. I signed on to this job as Mom for Life, and she will just have to put up with me. It won't be forever.

FOUR

KITH 'N' KIN

STILL DEAD?

DECEMBER 1995

amily and folks. Our kin, our relatives, our gang. The bunch, the lot, the litter, the whole kit 'n' kaboodle. Thanksgiving, Chanukah, Christmas, whatever. 'Tis the season, and we're all at home for the holidays.

At my house, a well-lighted Menorah and gluttonous attacks on potato pancakes piled high with sour cream and apple sauce. Across the street, twinkling lights in every tree and gluttonous attacks on turkey and ham.

God, what sumptuous scenes of familial fun, brotherly love, sisterly serenity, children with their faces aglow and mother . . . uh, Mother? Where the hell is Mother?

I look around thinking she – the mother, the mom, la madre, the real star of these family holidays – is just about to waddle out of the bedroom, gray hair sleep-flattened against her head, huddled under her ancient chenille bathrobe – the old, worn kind with the fluffy cotton lumps all over it, not today's smooth, silky, expensive kind.

She is just turning around from her station in front of the oven, waving a spatula at me and giggling, "So? Don't just stand there! Get busy grating those potatoes."

She is wrapping my Chanukah gifts.

"Books, what else? Why not learn something, for a change, instead of just giving in to all those ridiculous fashion fads," she says.

She is arguing, and losing, with my dad.

"A Christmas tree? Are you crazy? Guess what? We're not Christians. We don't celebrate Christmas. OK, OK. At least hide it in the den, away from the front windows in case the rabbi drives past."

She has put off shopping too long, has dragged me along and now we are lost in a parking lot. She has no idea where her car is.

"You see?" she moans. "This is why I hate cars. This is why I hate malls. They're all alike, so confusing, so dangerous. Oh, there it is!"

"That one?" I shriek. "The one with the stupid plastic flower taped to the antenna? Oh, Mother, how embarrassing."

"We found the car, didn't we?"

My mother has been dead for six years, and I think it's time for her to stop.

Admittedly, this has been an interesting phase, this dead part, but enough is enough. We experienced a difficult but dignified death, a cathartic coping period, a normal grieving phase.

Then we had a lot of silence, during which time we heard not a word from you.

During this, the holiday season, I get occasional communiqués, mostly having to do with your unearthly observations that I am spoiling my children, cooking the latkes in too much fat and, as always, doing too much.

"My God! Don't you ever stop? Sit down, put your feet up, tell me EVERYthing."

Beginning about Year Five A.M. (After Mom) I actually wanted to tell her everything. Now I'll talk, I thought. But just show up, will ya? The novelty of this death-is-part-of-life stuff has worn off.

I'd love to know what you think about my new kitchen and my old husband. And how 'bout that Madeleine Albright — wow! A woman secretary of state!

Have you heard the debate about butter vs. margarine? Can you believe your grandson is six feet tall? Do you like my hair short or long? Any opinion about estrogen replacement therapy? And get a load of my daughter's retro fashion look. Oh, so excuse me. I forgot you turned your nose up at polyester in 1968, so you're probably asking, "What's to like now?"

Please bring the recipe for sweet potato casserole, including the cooking time. I burn it every year. Bring that long-running list of everything you've done since last we talked but forgot to mention to me and, oh yeah, bring some more books.

Also, I'd like to know where you've been the last six years. Did you finally get a good night's sleep? Can you still hear Daddy snoring? Do they put candles on the Menorah up there or still use that same old vessel of oil? Are we in trouble for having the tree in the den?

It's time to knock it off, Mother. We're all home for the holidays, and you're no where to be found. Just come on down, we always have plenty of food. Besides, I'd much rather see you at the holidays than when I look in the mirror.

GOTCHA, SIS
JUNE 2004

ometime during the early Sixties, my younger sister and I were introduced to Hostess Cupcakes. The credit surely belonged to Mom who tossed the plastic-wrapped chocolate mounds onto the kitchen table in front of us straight from the grocery bag she was emptying.

Hostess turned their cupcakes out in two flavors: Vanilla, a wan-looking yellow cakey thing with brownish icing — ick — or chocolate, our favorite. Rich, dark chocolate with chocolate icing. Each of the twin cupcakes was filled with a white blob of so-called cream and was decorated with the trademark squiggling line of white icing that glazed the sugary chocolate top.

Customarily, I opened the package and moved the now-exposed cupcakes resting on a flimsy piece of flat, white cardboard toward the middle of the table so the game of Mutual Sister Torturing could begin.

I remember sitting on a sticky vinyl chair on hot summer days, stretching out over the yellow linoleum-top table, leaning my head onto the crook of my arm. That angle put me at about eye level with the cupcakes, but most importantly, I was looking down at my younger, shorter sister. I was always above her, always at an advantage, the privilege, after all, of the older sister.

Naturally, I went first, choosing the cupcake I wanted based on which of the two had the biggest globs of dripping chocolate down its sides. My mother must have put an end to that because somewhere along the way, I had to give the kid turns at being first.

But nothing was enough for her — my devilish, maddening sister — who glared at me strategically, as I chomped mindlessly into my cupcake, taking it all down in big bites. Hands in her lap, chin barely grazing the tabletop, eyes gazing up at me, she waited. Not until I broke for a glass of milk, with only a little piece of my treat left to eat, did she begin her psych op.

Slowly, her arm came out from under the table to pick up her cupcake.

Carefully, she peeled off the icing, her goal a perfect, all-in-one piece of frosting.

Pointedly, she laid the smooth, gritty chocolate circle on her plate.

Then, without so much as a nod toward my nearly empty plate, she ate her naked cupcake, scooping the cream out with her finger, never bothering with the distraction of milk. God, she was a smart one.

Her cupcake was now gone, but the prize — the icing — was still in one piece, and again she sat and waited, still and sure armed, until I had finished my entire cupcake.

Then, and only then, after she could be sure I had nothing more to eat, would she lift her large, round disk of dark icing and eat it slowly and smugly, bite by bite.

Slapping my palm onto the table, barking, "I hate you!" I left the kitchen, furious and bested, but never admitting it.

Many years and many cupcakes later, I see that she had to indulge herself in this small victory over me. What else can a younger sister do? Lording it over her was my particular talent and the birthright of the first-born. But she started out behind, so catch-up and gotcha were all she had.

When we played school, I was the teacher, she the stupid student. Office? I was the boss, she the tyrannized secretary. We even played library — I was the powerful librarian, she the inanimate book. I chose every game and called every shot.

Equality does not apply to sisters; somebody has to lead the other one by the nose. The Brontes deferred to Charlotte; the Andrews Sisters fell apart without LaVerne. Years are years; older and younger don't change.

But I am no longer looming, nor is she the kid I was stuck with. In fact, I'm glad to have the brat around. Helpful and encouraging, she's careful of my soft spots, holding her tongue when she knows it would hurt. We've each had lots of victories, but no longer in games with each other. Now we're more a duo than duelers, more teammates than taunters.

Nobody can unleash bellyaching laughter in us like we can for each other. Nobody can sound a silent alarm with that raised-eyebrow look of caution at the other. My sister, my pal, my partner in crime.

Now strung together by cells and cell phones, under-cooking the turkey or howling at a mountain moon. Occasionally, I still try to run the business, be the boss. Occasionally, she still holds out on the icing. But Lord help the mister — father, husband or son — that comes between me and my sister. And Lord help the sister who comes between … well, never mind that part.

THE MAESTRO
JUNE 1999

y father is a musician of sorts.

Not to mislead you, he doesn't sing or play an instrument. He doesn't compose or conduct music. He can't even whistle very well. But he does make music.

On a wall in his home in Dallas a brass plaque reads, "Bud's Conservatory," and just beyond the plaque a door opens into a closet.

It's a small closet, stacked ceiling to floor with stereo and recording equipment, CDs, records, cassette tapes and labels. Just a closet to most of us, but a world of pleasure to my dad, Bud.

In this spot, Bud makes music. For more than 85-plus years of life, he has channeled his enjoyment of music into this mini recording-studio-in-a-closet. In the Conservatory (hah!) he plays CDs for hours, listening to sounds old and new, operatic and swing, vocalists and soft jazz, Broadway and boogie.

His own collection is enormous, but listening is not all he does. From his ever-growing collection, he selects tunes and numbers that describe an era or capture a particular artist or simply reflect what he likes. Then he compiles his selections, records them on audio cassettes — complete with informative and historical commentary by, of course, Bud himself — and mails them to family and friends.

At first he made tapes just for my sister and me. Now he makes them by the dozens for us and for friends around the country. He keeps them catalogued and even takes orders and requests. Each tape comes with his typed "music notes," listings and personal comments.

He's made several Big Band tapes, selections — his, of course — from Tommy Dorsey, Glenn Miller and Duke Ellington. After Ella Fitzgerald died, Bud sent me his tribute tape to her, beginning where she began with "A Tisket a Tasket."

He enjoys great arias, too, and now so can I, as the tapes accompany me on errands back and forth between work and home, between Oklahoma and Texas, between my life with Bud and my life since.

My favorites are his. He's up to "Bud's Favorites No. 12," 15 tunes including Nat King Cole's "Paradise," Sinatra's "The Second Time Around," "Tangerine" from Helen O'Connell (who?), and "Lazy River" by Hoagy Carmichael.

When Ol' Blue Eyes died, Bud made two tribute tapes: one of Frank's Broadway songs, one of his ballads. Bud can't get too much of Frank. His intro on one Sinatra tape goes like this: "This tape is for our friends Helen and Bob Schmidt. Helen says 'I'll Never Smile Again' is her favorite, so I found this version by Frank Sinatra and the Pied Pipers with the Tommy Dorsey Orchestra from 1945. So get ready for ol' Frankie Boy, Helen. Hope you enjoy it!"

Bud is a long, tall Texan with Panhandle sensibilities, a terrific handicap, a still-working work ethic, bred-in-the-bone optimism, a gentle love his family never doubts, and a way of coping with anything life hands him with an always-ready sense of humor. Except for the golf swing, I have learned everything I need to know from him.

He learned these values in a less complicated world, America in the Thirties, Forties and Fifties. Then music and entertainment were sweet, funny and carefree, and life felt more like soft shoe than heavy metal. Benny Goodman and Margaret Whiting lulled soldiers to sleep at night; Jack Benny and Bob Hope kept them laughing all day. Gangsta Rap didn't help then or now, because in spite of great calamity, Americans had the sun in the morning and the moon at night.

Father's Day came around this year, and after talking to Bud, I realized the gifts come from him. Better than the man who reaches into his pocket and hands his kids candy, or the flashy, raucous Dallasite who doles out stiff, new stock certificates, my Dad reaches into his conservatory, pulls out a tape and says, "I made this for you."

Bud's musical sidebars arrive as gifts for me. If I'm blue, maybe overwhelmed with my own job as a parent, I have only to slip one of his Favorites into my tape player and listen to Judy Garland (or could it be Bud?) telling me to forget my troubles, come on get happy.

EPILOGUE

On my dad's 90th birthday, we gathered friends and family and had a snazzy party at a nice joint in his hometown of Dallas. A week before, he sent my sister and me a custom-made recording of seven versions of the Twenties Hoagy Carmichael classic, "Stardust." The whole disc. One song done seven ways.

He recorded renditions from Frank Sinatra, Ella Fitzgerald, Louis Armstrong, Wynton Marsalis, Artie Shaw, Nat King Cole and Hoagy himself, each version performed differently with my dad's own narration and his remembrance of the song or performer between each track.

"This one is ol' Satchmo," he said into the microphone, speaking of Armstrong.

Then: "Here we go with Ella. What a doll!"

His favorite is Frank Sinatra's adaptation. Ol' Blue Eyes sings only the song's introduction, a plaintive, poetic overture that leaves you longing for the refrain. Who would have thought Sinatra would choose to do the song this clever way? Who would have thought that my dad, a pretty straight-forward guy, would especially like this off-note version? And how would I have ever known about this treasure without his carefully collected gift to me?

Me, a Sixties kid, a lover of the Beatles, Chuck Berry, Martha and the Vandellas.

At the birthday party, we played the "Stardust" collection on the res-taurant's stereo as background music, setting just the right mood.

At 92, Bud is still burning away at his music station, sending CDs by snail mail to friends, old and young. (He abandoned cassette tapes when the recording industry did, and made the transition to CDs easily, updat-

ing his equipment and labeling techniques. He's still a damn good engineer, loving all things electronic.)

My dad has given me many things, but this gift — seven ways of hearing one beautiful song — is one of my favorites.

A LITTLE MORE POP

FEBRUARY 1998

I n 1902, a 12-year-old French-German boy and his 13-year-old sister left their home in Alsace-Lorraine and traveled by ship to America with nothing but the clothes they were wearing and the name of a man who might give them a job.

Eventually, the boy, Felix Mandell, settled in Texas, not far from another sister and brother who had immigrated some years earlier. His sister, Camille, found her way to New Mexico. But they never saw their parents again.

What Felix did see was 98 years of life that stretched from 1890 to 1988, from a tiny village in Europe to a hot, sprawling cow town in the American West, from that lonely trip across the sea to a family and friends who would surround and adore him the rest of his long life.

He died last week, my grandfather Pop, just hours after winning a big pot – about $2.50 – in his weekly poker game. He had not been sick or in pain. He had his disappointments, to be sure, and like most immigrants, he knew dislocation and struggle, loneliness and the feelings of an outsider. But as with many Europeans who settled in the West, America and Americans were good to him. By leaving Europe, he and his family escaped the destruction of European Jewry, bringing their hope and faith to a new world.

He had, very simply, just lived, and for him it was enough. *"C'est suffit,"* he said to me often and about many things. "It's enough."

I think that attitude may have been the reason he lived so long and so well. He never went to school after the fourth grade in France; he never learned to drive a car; he never owned a home or jewelry or furs or traveled much. Yet whatever he did or had was enough for him. He had his health, his love of baseball, a good job, a decent living, a family and many friends. He lived all of his adult life in the dusty, flat, but friendly town of Amarillo, Texas.

And he did see two brothers named Wright try to lift a plane out of a field in Chicago one afternoon in the early 1900s. He saw the Chicago White Sox play in their heyday. He raised a son who graduated from college and became his lifelong companion. He was there for the births of his grandchildren and even great-grandchildren.

For 40 years he sold mens' hats in Amarillo to friends and customers who came to the store as much for his charm and good nature as his handling of haberdashery.

"A man's not dressed without a hat," he'd say, never accepting the trend for men to appear bare-headed in public.

His days were simple, his needs uncomplicated, his humor warm and easy. His attitudes were tolerant, forgiving, hopeful and loving. His eyes smiled, his moustache twitched, his arms opened and everyone loved Pop.

Living modestly, he traveled through the Dust Bowl, the Depression and two world wars with no more baggage than he brought off that ship.

I don't think I can live like my Pop, coasting along, moving gently through time. But some days, when I barely have time to come up for air and everything I've always wanted isn't nearly enough, I hope that sheer genetics will prevail. I could do well with a little more of Pop.

PEANUTS AND CRACKER JACKS

I t only took me a few pitches to fall in love with Mark Gardner. The starter for the San Francisco Giants kept the Chicago Cubs scoreless until the fifth inning of the one-game playoff for the National League wild card playoff slot, and though the Cubs were my team, I liked Gardner's dark, wavy hair and chiseled features.

The camera came in close. On the mound, he looked worried, but still tough and, I thought, great. Strong, bright eyes. Young but not silly. Loved the way his cap came down over his forehead.

He turned his head, and I got a better look at the aqualine profile.

Then he spit. But he didn't just spit. He actually wound up for the spit, turning his head way back over one shoulder, bringing it back to center and, with speed at least half that of his fastball, he let it sail, this hideous glob of whatever it was.

Oh, brother. That drove out Gardner — both for San Francisco and for me. Call me fickle, but call me finished with that spitter.

By now my attention was more on the game and less on the guy, anyway. Cubs' hitter Gary Gaetti broke the scoreless game wide open with a two-run homer followed by a triumphant bow from the dugout. Wow! Those loveable losers may get there yet!

What a hit! What a hitter! What a guy!

With fans cheering, "Guy-ett-tee! Guy-ett-tee!" he modestly returned to the dugout, sat down next to one of his teammates and exchanged a nod and two shakes. And then the two of them started to chew.

And chew they did. I found myself rubbing my own aching jaw watching in astonishment as they chewed and chewed, faster and faster, heads still but jaws a-pumpin'.

Gaetti has just broken this game wide open bringing his team back to life and these two just sit there like zombies and chew? Yech.

Cubs pitcher Steve Trachsel takes his time between pitches so the camera roams a lot. At this point, we got a nice shot of the Giants' dugout and Armando Rios — not a bad-looking fellow himself. Rios was leaning back against the wall, arms crossed in front, and I was fully enjoying the view. Then he stretched out, put his hands behind his head and after easily five full seconds of major league chewing, he blew the biggest, pinkest bubble I've ever seen.

At least you could see what he was chewing.

Another break, and we got a close-up of Orel Hirshiser, that sweet boy from Buffalo. I remembered when he was an all-American hero. An ace pitcher, Cy Young Award winner and a great all-around athlete. What a charming young man, I mused. I guessed Orel must not be playing much because he had on his shiny black Giants jacket, was sitting off to one side of the dugout kind of by himself and was, you got it, chewing.

But Orel was being much more than oral. He would reach down (below the screen) and — without even looking down! — toss something into his mouth. Once in his mouth, whatever it was got chewed up a little, spit out and in would go more. What the hell is that? I asked myself, squinting and edging closer to the TV. Peanuts? Was he shelling them with his teeth? Popcorn? Was he spitting out the kernels? Sure I was impressed with his eye-hand coordination, but more than a little grossed out.

By now the game was getting hot. The Giants were trailing 4-0 with two outs and the bases loaded. Manager Dusty Baker must have been tense, but the only sign was the toothpick he alternately chewed and flipped in and out of his mouth or balanced between his uppers and lowers. While I worried about the toothpick, he worried about the game.

Barry Bonds was up next. He's big, he's calm and he's got a cool earring. A choker in postseason, he'd been a great hitter and the Giants' best hope to get back in the game. I moved up to the edge of my seat.

Before Bonds gets into position, we see a lot of him. Against the background of the darkening Chicago sky. Warming up with two bats. The camera loves him at every angle and especially in close on this boyishly handsome powerhouse.

And at that pivotal moment when we see every pore and bead of sweat on his face, guess what? He spits, too. At least Gardner turned to one side. Highlighted by the combined luminosity of the television and the ballpark lights, Bonds just lets loose with full frontal spew. His slimy blast is long and hard and accompanied by an exploding spray.

After this show, his at-bat was anti-climactic for me. The three-time MVP grounded out to first, then, in another display of class and good taste, he slammed his helmet to the ground.

Epilogue

I'm writing this afterthought on Aug. 8, 2007, the day Barry Bonds broke Hank Aaron's career home run record and hit his 756th homer into the stands at AT&T Park for the San Francisco Giants.

"I move over and offer my best wishes to Barry and his family on this historical achievement," Aaron said in a videotaped message to Bonds that was broadcast over the ballpark's video screen. "My hope today, as it was on that April evening in 1974, is that the achievement of this record will inspire others to chase their own dreams."

The message, shown to 42,154 people in the stadium, "means absolutely everything," said Bonds, the 43-year-old who had earlier slugged his way past Willie Mays' mark of 660 homers, then surpassed Babe Ruth's total of 714 home runs.

Bonds is certainly controversial, bullishly standing up to suspicions of illegal steroid use for years, causing friction between him and baseball commissioner Bud Selig and leaving many baseball fans dissatisfied. Unproven steroid use isn't the only thing that has turned some off to Bonds. As he approached this record-breaking event, his arrogance was unattractive, especially compared to the humility Aaron and Mays —

Bonds' godfather – displayed throughout their careers. Ruth, as it turns out, abused alcohol much of his life. But alcohol wasn't illegal in sports, and we didn't know much about his drinking anyway.

All of which makes spitting and helmet tossing and even yelling at umpires seem like peanuts. But the days of ballplayers serving as role models are hard to remember, Cal Ripken Jr. aside. Blame the money, blame the owners, blame the players.

However the debates about money-soaked professional athletics and steroid use come out, Bonds has been hitting that baseball long, hard and far, and a record breaker is a record breaker. As Giants manager Bruce Bochy said, "The fact of the matter is, that's a lot of home runs."

I talked to one Manhattan-based TV sports producer, Joey Fleischaker, my favorite son, who gave Bonds this, "Steroid use or not, he stood at the plate and outsmarted the pitcher 756 times … He is also the most 'walked' batter in all of baseball, so he only saw a select amount of pitches to hit – far fewer than any other player in the game – and he still hit those out of the park. Imagine if he'd gotten more pitches to hit."

THE GUTS TO VOTE

SEPTEMBER 1998

I like unusual gifts. Not unusual like baby cheetahs or a trek in the Himalayas or a new Smith & Wesson but still, unusual. For example, when my son became 18, I hauled him down to a tag agency and asked him to register to vote. It took 20 minutes, total. I told him that, along with some CDs, this was his gift: his right to vote. We live freely, every day, I reminded both of us, because we can vote for or against the people who make our laws.

The value of this gift may not be obvious. But it may be the most valuable gift you ever get, I said. Your freedom — all of ours — depends on it. Please use it.

So, naturally, when my birthday came long, I hauled same son out of bed and this time drove him to a polling place.

The primary election this year in Oklahoma happened to be the day before my birthday. I want you to vote, I told him. Knowing that you voted, that you have actually done your duty, is the gift I want from you.

"Who do I vote for?" he asked. "Isn't it just a primary?"

I handed him the Oklahoma Gazette's special section on judicial races and The Sunday Oklahoman's voter guide.

"Read this," I said. "It's not everything, but it's something. And a primary sets up the fall election. Maybe we can get rid of some useless incumbents."

"Don't I need I.D?"

"Nope. It's easy. You're already registered. You just walk in, give your name, vote. They make it easy to vote in Oklahoma. So there's no reason not to."

We drove five blocks, parked and walked only about 30 yards to the entrance to Horace Mann School, the polling place for our precinct, gave our names, got our ballots, filled them out, put them in the counting machine, slapped "I Voted!" stickers to our lapels, and that was it.

In only about 10 minutes — maybe 20, if you count the time it took to "become informed" — we had exercised that most basic of all democratic rights and most important responsibility. We had done something for our own freedom no less significant than what the president is doing by meeting with Boris Yeltsin or what Janet Reno is doing by examining alleged violations of campaign finance laws or what embassy employees are doing by risking their lives to serve the goals of democracy in East Africa.

We had given our consent to be governed, no small power that. But my son and I were among the measly 21 percent of registered voters in the state who accepted that responsibility, enjoyed that power and cast our votes on Aug. 25. That was the lowest voter turnout in a gubernatorial primary in Oklahoma in 50 years, matching a trend nationwide.

Oh, those politicians don't care what we think, you say, giving a reason for not voting. They only listen to money, big money, the media, each other, whatever. Why bother? They're corrupt, out of touch, amoral, immoral, dishonest, disconnected, irrelevant, out of line and you're out of patience with all of it

The economy's fine, you can't connect to politics, anyway, so you don't vote. Besides, there's nobody good to vote for.

Baloney. Lots of smart, hardworking, caring men and women are still running for office. Not everyone is disillusioned with public service or American politics. By not voting, you let them down. They have the guts to run; at least you can have the guts to vote.

These are not good reasons, they're excuses. If you just stay home and watch the people you complain about run, win, hold office and get re-elected, that is exactly what will happen. Some would even say you get who you deserve.

Don't you imagine that if, instead of 21 percent, 95 percent actually voted, you'd see politicians listening to those voters and not just their consultants?

That's the way it's supposed to work, the way it was meant to work and the only way it can work. Someone will govern, whether you like them or not, whether you get up off your can and do something about it or not.

Want to see what government and politics is like in America without the freedom and responsibility to vote? You are.

EPILOGUE

My son, Joey Fleischaker, now 24, did more than just vote in Oklahoma's 1998 primary election. In the 2000 presidential election campaign, he made himself useful to the managers of the Democratic National Convention in Los Angeles. That job then evolved into a four-month assignment in the Gore-Lieberman campaign traveling ahead of vice presidential candidate U.S. Sen. Joe Lieberman, D-Conn., on the advance staff, setting up meetings, rallies, press events and motorcades in cities across the country. He learned – from the inside out – what real politics in America is about.

He crisscrossed the country, worked hard, slept little, ate junk on the run, was abused by power-hungry politicians and their power-hungry staff, or abandoned by inept campaign workers unused to the pressure, and I think he loved every minute of it. He's young, hungry himself and ready to rock 'n' roll. Not many of his contemporaries voted in this election, but I am proud to say that he did.

FIVE

TRUFFLES AND TRUSSES

GORGING ON GRAS
JANUARY 1996

aybe it was our cruising altitude of 30,000 feet. Maybe it was the sheer headiness of the luxury of traveling business class, but I had a dream somewhere over the Atlantic between the Strait of Denmark and the Labrador Sea from which I awakened terrified at the sound of my coronary arteries slamming shut.

I dreamed I was swimming – slogging, really – across the Seine, that muddied band of a river flowing oh, so romantically, so bittersweetly, so very Frenchly through Paris.

But wait. My Seine was not running with clear water, sparkling water, Evian or even Parisian sewage. The river of my dreams was nearly oozing with *foie gras.*

In my fancy, I was not only stuffed with this rich and distinctly European delight (*la femme farcie de foie gras*), I was totally surrounded by it (*foie gras en croute*), slicing through it (*foie gras farci*), and finally, drowning in it (*la mort par foie gras*).

No Freudian analyst need interpret this dream. I was returning from a week in France with my family, where we individually and collectively put away more thick slices of *foie gras* than there are guillotined revolutionary heads stockpiled at the Bastille.

When the first waiter at the first meticulously selected restaurant brought our first plates of this gastronomic treat, four sets of American eyes squinted with doubt. Clearly, this was not the chopped liver of Bar Mitzvah fame (made with bourgeois chicken livers); not really paté (much chunkier); and certainly not Oscar Mayer's liverwurst sausage (yuck). This, then, was something else; something to live and, quite possibly, die for.

Foie gras translates from French to English as "fat liver" and translates visually from a slice of meatloaf to a slice of smooth, creamy, artistically blended paste of fattened goose or duck liver, cut to about one-half inch thickness and "crusted" with a great, golden glob of greasy, gelatinous goosey fat.

Foie gras is absolutely delicious in its unique, velvety way. It has the texture of smooth, ultra-rich butter laced with a mild gamy taste and enhanced, sometimes, by patterning the liver in stripes, squares or harlequins.

Foie gras apparently originated with the Egyptians in 2500 B.C. and is made by forcing geese and ducks to eat more than they normally would, a process perfected by nearly every American in Paris. Who knows what's happening to our livers, but the livers of these birds just get larger and larger and more and more succulent.

"The result," says David Rosengarten in the "Dean and DeLuca Cookbook," "is a creamy, fatty, ultra-seductive chew that sends a shiver down the spine of most diners."

I'll say. I've seen the spines of my diners — one teen-ager and one post — shiver over nachos, pizza or a Quarter Pounder with cheese, and their noses turn skyward at the mention of liver 'n' onions. But even these gringos were gorging on the *gras*.

In Paris, we were stuffed with *foie gras* before our entrees every single night for six successive nights. And on the seventh night, we rested. Actually, we kept on eating like the gluttonous little American piggies we had become — *crepes, coquilles, terrines, éclairs, brioche,* etc. — but on more *foie gras*, we declared a moratorium which lasted for all of one day, until we arrived in Alsace-Lorraine, home to the foiest of all gras. There we hoarded tins of it to cart home.

When those are gone, we'll be left to our own devices. I'm told they serve *foie gras* here in the city — made with imported goose liver — at La Baguette and sometimes at The Coach House. I wish I didn't know that.

Should we want to try rustling up some at home, we won't find organ donors. The practice of pumping up goose livers is prohibited in the United States. But one can buy whole fattened duck livers from the distributor, D'Artagnan (honest) at 1-973-344-0565 or from Dean & DeLuca's Web site, www.deandeluca.com.

I can't say enough wonderful things about this blend. It has the capacity to stop all conversation, to bring out the pride of French chefs. One refused to bring us bread before serving his own *foie gras* course produced from his own gaggle, lest we fill up on the bread first. It has the effect of inducing a kind of eyelid-drooping, sensual torpor on its gourmands, as the luscious liver melts in your mouth with the result, no doubt, of taking five years off your life.

So who cares? *C'est la vie avec foie gras.* Let's all revise our living wills. Leave Dr. Kevorkian at home. Life and death, please, by gorging on *gras*.

PANTYHOSE BUYER SHOPS 'TIL SHE DROPS

JULY 1991

ne size never has fit all. One size, in fact, has never fit me at all, but just when I thought I'd give it another try, an industry left unregulated for too long has shaken the very legs on which I stand.

I speak, miserably, of pantyhose. Enter the hosiery section of any department store and see if you, too, aren't brought absolutely to your knees by the impossible task of buying some.

My favorite shopping sidekick and I ran into our local department store just to pick up some off-white ones, with maybe a little pattern. I should have smelled trouble when my buddy asked me about my membership in The Club. I have known this woman for years. We are both Democrats, the Junior League wouldn't have us, and Ellie Smeal burned our NOW cards years ago. I didn't know what club she meant.

"The Hosiery Club," she said. "It's great. Buy 12, get another pair free."

This club is certainly no support group; it is a scheme to make crazy every pantyhose buyer in America. Buy 12 pair of pantyhose? Twelve double-legged harnesses chosen from case after case of daunting options? Who would want 12 pair?

Style offerings alone include silky, silky-sheer, opaque, support, light support, reinforced toe, reinforced heel, sandalfoot, control top, light control top, bikini top, cotton crotch or any combination of the above. All this just to cover a few spider veins and cinch in a little cellulite.

And we're just getting to color, of which there are hundreds, described for example as "ecru," "snowflake" or "crystal" but never just "off-white."

On to size, which includes "A," fitting everyone from pre-Kindergarten to newlywed; "B," which claims to work for ladies weighing anywhere from 110 to 150 pounds, no matter how short or how shaped; and "C" or "D," for gals who would be better off buying a giant Ace bandage and wrapping it around their thighs, because that's how queen-sized panty-hose worn by anyone other than queens feel anyway.

Now, remember. I just want off-white with a little something in the way of pattern. Too soon I learn I can have dots, pinstripes, big stripes, chevrons, squares, squiggles, lines up the back, bows on the heel, rhine-stones on the ankle. Flo Nightingale white is available, but apparently the one thing I cannot have is just a *little* pattern.

Taking in row after row of hosiery counters, my knees start to knock, I grab my package (one pair, one big gamble) which costs half my pay-check, and I flee, glad my bare legs are still working.

Another friend says she finds the shopping part not as bad as the wearing-them part.

"There are so many humiliations," she says, "like roll-at-the-top syn-drome, contracted when you buy 'B' but should have bought 'C,' and the pantyhose slip down and last night's dinner is pushed up. I even went back to wearing a garter belt," she confessed.

"But that experiment failed the day my garters came unsnapped, loud-ly and painfully, in a management meeting."

Occasionally, hosiery sales ladies are willing to help you with the fine art of getting them on and off.

"Sit down, dear," says a woman you suspect cuts them off at the knees and rolls 'em down.

"Start with one foot (duh) and pull, pull, pull! until you have reached the knee, then begin with the other foot."

I'm already feeling pain at the pull, pull, pull part when she finishes off with, "Now we're halfway there so wiggle left! and pull! Right! Pull! Now, pull evenly and, voila! You're in!"

In and totally exhausted, I should add, and you haven't even started on the strapless bra.

There is one last pantyhose problem yet to be solved by industry – one shared equally, for once, by women and men. Getting into them in a hurry is bad enough, but getting out?

Edward Scissorhands, where are you when we need you?

CONFESSIONS OF A CHOCOHOLIC

FEBRUARY 1991

L ike any addiction, it consumes. Between fixes, I feel sad and
lethargic.

I can't keep it at home because I can't be trusted. So late at
night I roam the streets of my neighborhood trying to score
off my friends. I heard there was a huge supply unloaded in
Norman, Okla., last weekend, but I had to be locked up to stay away.

Why should I shake this habit? Of all my personal "isms" – cynicism,
neuroticism, astigmatism, Judaism, feminism, liberalism – my favorite is
chocoholism.

I am wild about, obsessed with, driven madly toward and made totally
nuts by my intense and predictable cravings for chocolate. I don't just like
or want chocolate. I really, really love it. And I really, really need it. I think
about it a lot. I arrange private time to slip out and buy one – one can't
hurt, can it? – chocolate turtle.

I am quick to accept party invitations from hostesses who are known
for their chocolate bundt cakes or brownies. I steal Halloween bags from
children, sorting out all the mini-Snickers, Milky Ways, Kisses and
M&Ms. I go on Easter egg hunts if there's any hope of unearthing chocolate eggs, and I make sure to exchange holiday gifts with highly acclaimed
fudge makers. Fudge, oh God. The best.

Now why is an already chubby girl like me double-fisting this stuff?
One explanation is genetic coding. For centuries, my grandfather's family
supplied its French village with rich, gooey *mousse au chocolate, gateau
chocolate* and *chocolate parfait.* So who am I to deny this luscious lineage?

But time and over-breeding have diluted the familial continental pal-
ate, and I don't require Godiva, Neuhaus or even Toblerone. Oh, I like
them, all right. *Mon dieu!*

But mine is the American way, and I am just as happy with a Hershey Bar, Nestles Crunch, Hostess chocolate cream-filled cupcakes, Double Stuff Oreos – hell, I'm happy with regular-sized Oreos – or Chips Ahoy. Strike the Ahoy. I eat the chips. I do get desperate.

"Hello?" I am panting through the phone late at night to my understanding friend and neighbor. "Do you have anything chocolate?"

She searches. "Only chocolate syrup," she says. "You know, for the kids' milk."

I steal out into the night carrying my spoon. The kids can drink plain milk.

Our city, oft-criticized for its limitations, does have rich, hidden treasures of chocolate ecstasy dotting the landscape like dark jewels, and believe me, I know where to find most of them.

Try Fudge Love at the 42nd Street Candy Store; chocolate donuts at the Donut Shop N.W. 63rd and Western; Chocolate Chewies at Ingrid's; brownies at ND Foods or the Urban Market; the chocolate bomb at Flip's; Devil's food birthday cake with fudge icing from Kamp's; chocolate-filled chocolate *éclairs* at La Baguette; or my grandma's Texas pecan Mexican chocolate sheet cake with fudge frosting at my house.

By the way, don't even mention white chocolate to me. Cooked up by some honky Pharisee, it is a pale pretender of the real thing.

If I've missed anything, by all means, let this chocoholic know.

Epilogue

Since I confessed my consuming chocolate passion, I've heard from many of you.

None advocate recovery.

None want to be clean.

None want to endure the sobering experience of a life without chocolate.

Happily, this addiction instead of rotting your liver turns out to be good for you, at least in some forms.

In the last five years, dark chocolate has become the new health food. Hurray! A justification for my sins! Believed to be high in antioxidants, studies have shown (don't you love that authoritative line, "Studies have shown … ") – dark chocolate, not milk or white chocolate, no, no, no – lowers blood pressure, improves blood flow and does all the other good stuff antioxidants do. And apparently, the darker the better.

What to look for? Cocoa percentages should be high, very high. Of course, capitalism being what it is, there are now endless varieties of dark chocolate concoctions where before we were just content with a bag of M&Ms.

Speaking of those yummy little discs – and why shouldn't we – obsession is, after all, obsessive. I wouldn't think of turning down a bittery-rich, expensive Scharffenberger, Godiva or Ghirardelli's Twilight Delight. But I certainly will not turn my nose up at M&Ms, either. In fact, that's my newest recommendation. If you can't be contented with M&Ms, honey, you're hopeless.

I guess a plain brown package of milk chocolate M&Ms got to be old hat. Responding immediately to market demand, the folks at Mars now offer you a yellow package – M&M Peanut; or the new purple bag, Dark Chocolate M&Ms – and combos. The latest are: Dark Chocolate M&M Peanut (purple and yellow package); Almond M&Ms (tan); RaZZberry; Peanut Butter; M&M Mints; Baking Bits and Customized M&Ms.

Customized M&Ms? Shut up!!!! But please do take my advice here. Before reading another word, click onto www.mymms.com and order M&Ms with any message in any color you want for any one you want. Want to be an enabler at Christmas time? You can custom design M&Ms in red and green and with a religious message, too, if that floats your boat. I was sent huge bags of blue and white, Menorah-embossed M&Ms for Chanukah last year from the pusher in the family (she only likes fruit candy) and I made myself silly and sick over them.

But lest you think I am all about mass-produced chocolate, it's my duty to tell you that here in Oklahoma, the Chickasaw Nation is producing "gourmet" chocolate called "Bedré" and selling it online. The milk chocolate molds of the Sooner State are a kick and a great dinner party place card, or try the chocolate-covered potato chips.

Bedré, located in Paul's Valley, Okla., also offers Oklahoma and Texas Cow Patties (yep, you read it right) or a white chocolate bison. Only in Oklahoma. www.bedrechocolates.com. You decide.

Elsewhere in the state, my co-addict in Tulsa reports Nouveau on S. Memorial makes wonderful truffles, and here in Oklahoma City, while we've lost the chocolate bomb at Flip's, Coco Flow makes out-of-this-world chocolate shortbread cookies, hot cocoa and beautiful chocolate candy. Coco Flow made its name with those three-tiered chocolate fountains flowing with rich, running chocolate, surrounded by fruit and cakes for dipping. A little hokey, yes, but very popular at office parties.

In a dark, needy moment, I'd have no problem lying down on the floor at a Chocoholics Anonymous meeting (the ChocALoco meeting) and telling my story.

"Hi. I'm Pam and I'm a chocoholic." Now let that chocolate fountain run all over me.

IT'S ME I'M LOOKIN' FOR

JANUARY 2007

ome on, admit it.

You've given some thought to cosmetic surgery. At least once? Maybe more than once?

I know I have. Clicking through pictures of my family playing in the sand and surf, I am puzzled. Who is that woman there with my children? It looks like my mother … she of the fallen face, missing eyelids and neck like a Thanksgiving turkey.

But it can't be my mother. She died 15 years ago with red rouge dotting her cheeks, hoping it would draw the visitor's eye up toward once-chiseled cheekbones instead of down toward lolling laugh lines.

No, no, no, that ain't her, babe. It's you.

It's me staring at the tracks of time on my face. Me who has more eyelid than eyes, more cheek than cheekbones. And it's me who rushes to the mirror for confirmation.

Oh, horrors! I'm right! The same person in the photo now stares back at me from my mirror.

My hands fly to my face, my eyes are wide (well, as wide as my eyes can get) with horror. With my thumbs, I hoist up my slumping skin, imagining all the extra stuff gone – who knows where, who cares, just gone.

I imagine it's been lifted, lasered, injected, collagened, Botoxed, Restylaned, derma-braised, nipped, tucked, lipo-ed or hypo-ed. Just somehow gotten the hell outta the way. How would I look then?

Better, I tell myself. (I have to move closer to the mirror at this point, to see what I'm doing.) Definitely. My face could look much better.

But wait! Look at that! Now my mouth looks worse. As I yank up my cheeks — uh oh — my mouth becomes thin, distended!

OK. Let's rearrange things, I murmur to myself, attempting composure. I scoot closer to the mirror, squint and inch my thumbs down just a little, aiming my mouth back where it started, but my Central and Upper Face still wilt. Presuming, that is, you can still call it a face with an overstretched mouth.

And all this might hurt, someone says to me from inside my head. That's a lot of skin to whack off. Hell, it might even kill me. It killed somebody who made it onto the cover, posthumously, of People magazine last year, didn't it?

Yet I hold the pose, considering my options.

Maybe I should also do something about these slits I call eyes. A surgeon once told me that my eyes were really the most offensive part of my aging skin problem. His name is Dr. No Tact, and he should not be on your list of consults.

To test the "Do-the-Eyes" theory, I leave my thumbs to the task of holding up some of the flagging face and lift the pelts under my eyebrows with my pinkies. The eyes are still too baggy, so I bring out my index fingers and add them to the makeshift winch.

Leaning over my bathroom sink, two inches from the mirror, hands and fingers splayed as if in a rendition of "Up in the Air, Junior Birdman," laughter overcomes me, a few new lines appear around my mouth, and I drop my hands and slap my thighs. (My thighs? Let's not even go there.)

You'll need a crane to fix this face, I tell myself, marching away from the mirror. Do cosmetic surgeons use cranes? And I haven't even gotten to my neck.

Author and screenwriter Nora Ephron feels bad about her neck and has written a best-seller saying so. She's trying to stop herself from going crazy as apparently many women (and some men) have, subjecting herself to one surgical or dermatological procedure after another.

One of my friends came to visit with a hole in her forehead the size of a minted California quarter, the result of a failed two-month-old Botox treatment. The worry lines on her forehead were gone, but believe me, she was still worried.

Mirror, mirror on the wall, am I just aging or living after all? I think I'll follow the advice of another friend who offers this: If you look in the mirror and think you need a face lift, maybe you're spending too much time in front of the mirror. Besides, I'm feeling just fine about my neck. It still holds up my head.

SIX

CONFESSIONS FROM A
WHITE HOUSE SLEEPOVER

CONFESSIONS FROM A WHITE HOUSE SLEEPOVER
MARCH 1997

PROLOGUE

In an attempt to convince the public that the president was cutting the corners of campaign finance laws, the Republican National Committee and its henchmen made a very big deal out of the Clintons' practice of inviting guests to spend the night at the White House and giving them the special privilege of staying in one of the formal guest rooms, the Lincoln Bedroom or the Queen's Bedroom.

This was in Clinton's first term when the GOPs couldn't have dreamed of what small trouble this flap was for Clinton compared to the big trouble he got into in his second term. But no matter. I was, and remain, a friend.

Some of those early Lincoln Bedroom guests were indeed major donors to the Democrats and to the president's re-election campaign, and that's how they got "found out."

I just proudly signed the guest book.

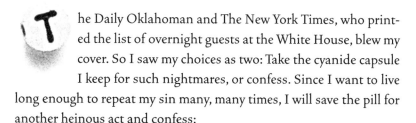

he Daily Oklahoman and The New York Times, who printed the list of overnight guests at the White House, blew my cover. So I saw my choices as two: Take the cyanide capsule I keep for such nightmares, or confess. Since I want to live long enough to repeat my sin many, many times, I will save the pill for another heinous act and confess:

I Spent a Night in the Lincoln Bedroom. By the way, I own the White House and all the bedrooms in it, as do you. We even own Lincoln's bed and all his old sheets, which I hope are changed frequently given how many people have been camping out there lately. But enough about the décor.

I Spent a Night at the White House for several reasons.

Public Reason: I was invited. I had plans to be in Washington, D.C., and wanted to spend some time with old friends, POTUS and FLOTUS[1] who are busy, busy, busy and had no other time to see me.

Hidden Reason: POTUS was attempting to lure me into using my vast influence to secure a $17 grillion contribution from our local conservative publishing family, the Gaylords, to either the Clinton-Gore re-election campaign or the Democratic National Committee.

Real Reason for Accepting: My schedule was also crowded. I was in D.C. to see old friends and to eat as many steamed Maryland blue crabs as I could find in one week. Being an old FOHAB[2], I also thought it would be fun to sit up and gab half the night with my friends.

Hidden Reason for Accepting: Secretly, clandestinely, passionately and most definitely in a calculated manner, I was hoping that Mandy Patinkin, Paul Newman or some other Hollywood don would mistakenly but luckily have been booked into the Lincoln Bedroom that same night. You see, there's only one bed. I know this because I went. Yes, indeedy, I did.

In fact, I spent 24 hours there, most of it alone and trying to sleep. For the record, the following should account for all of my time there:

8–11:30 P.M. I alternately and frequently read the Gettysburg Address and browsed through the guide booklet that explains the antiques in the Lincoln Bedroom. (In America, they're antiques. In Europe, they would be passed over at a flea market as too new.) I thought about playing "Chopsticks" or the "Rach

---

[1] President of the United States and First Lady of the United States
[2] Friend of Hillary's and Bill's

2" on the piano in the hallway, but was too nervous. I thought about snooping around other parts of the White House, but was too nervous. I thought about asking for food, but was too nervous, and wanted to call lots of my family and friends to tell them where I was, but was too nervous. So I read my crappy detective novel to calm myself and wondered where the hell my old friends were.

11:30–12:30 A.M. FLOTUS arrived. We had a nice talk about husbands, kids and jobs, and she went to bed.

12:30–1:30 A.M. POTUS arrived, found me snoring on a settee in the hallway and peeled the crappy detective novel off my nose. We put our feet up and sat around talking about kids, parents, jobs, our health, our friends and our enemies. He likes to talk more than she does, even more than I do. It was nice to have some time together.

1:30–7:30 A.M. Slept badly, clinging stiffly to four inches of Lincoln's bed and battling civil war ghosts. Awoke and ate my low-fat bagel with jam – ordered the night before and delivered with quiet style and unobtrusive elegance – drank decaffeinated coffee alone, read three important newspapers, showered and dressed. POTUS stopped by to say good-bye, see ya, and I left for my hotel, where I tried to get some sleep.

NOON Resumed the eating of steamed Maryland blue crabs with a mutual FOB and FOP.[3]

Neither Paul nor Mandy were at the White House, nor was any attempt made by anyone to tap into my well-known stash of $50,000–$100,000 campaign contributions.

We didn't talk about campaign finance reform, and I doubt POTUS, FLOTUS or the MOCs[4] will be either, at least in any meaningful way.

[3] Friend of Pam's
[4] Members of Congress

Power and greed are not solely the private properties of corporate America.

We did finally, the chief executive and I, have time to talk about the things real friends talk about so, in that way, I personally am glad POTUS was "ready to start the overnights … "

When Clinton and I and my husband and all of our mutual friends were kids just starting out in politics in Washington, we came and went from each other's houses all the time. But now he's living in a place with more security, and contrary to GOP opinion, it's hard to get a sleepover there: A fat check isn't enough. I tried to call Mr. Gaylord at his newspaper office when I returned to Oklahoma City to tell him the White House coffee is damned good, should he want to buy a cup for $17 grillion. He hasn't returned my call.

E P I L O G U E

A lot has happened to former President Bill Clinton and his wife Hillary since I spent that cold, windy night, alone in their guest bedroom. Historians can do a better job telling those tales, but I will tell you a short one of my own, which I have only recently remembered.

As I said, Hillary Clinton came to greet me, and we exchanged a few pleasantries before she went to bed. When she stood up to excuse herself, I sought her advice. Pathetic, I know, but I did.

"I've been waiting for a while to see Bill," I said, anxiously.

She nodded, motherly, understanding.

"He's very late," I said, "and I'm tired. If you were me, would you wait up for him?"

Today's leading candidate for president of the United States, now a U.S. senator from New York and then first lady of the U.S., Hillary threw her head back, laughed easily and said, "I've been asking myself that question all of my life. I'm afraid you're on your own there."

THROWING EGGS AT HAM

October 2003

I do not like Ahhnold the Ham,
I do not like the man he am.

I would not like him running our state
But praise the Lord,
That ain't our fate.
I do not like him here or there
But better California than anywhere.

I do not like him in a grope,
I would not, could not, with that dope.
On a movie set or in a gym
who would want
those hammy hands of him?

Ladies of all shape and kind,
Knew him well, up front and behind.
I would not want that in my house;
He behaved so bahhdly,
How dare he grouse?

I would not trust him spending my cash,
As he muscles his way to cut and slash.
I would not like his hands on my a**
Certainly not on my taxable stash.

Maria of Kennedy clan proclaimed
It's the chicks, not my Arnie who's to blame.
Trust me, she said; he's good for his word.
Vote for my beefcake, not the skinny
Gray nerd.

Out with the wimp! In with the buff!
When the votes were counted,
Ahhnold had enough
I would not have voted for that brawny guy
To him I say,
Hasta la vista, baby, bye-bye.

I would not give him
that much power
But now he is
the Hun of the Hour.

As with Reagan before
him, Californians might swoon,
And maybe Ahhnold can
restart the money boon.

If not, Golden Staters will just have to wait
For the next election this steroid
overdose to terminate.

Epilogue

Arnold Schwarzenegger did win the special election to follow Gray Davis as governor of California and was re-elected in 2006. To my surprise, he serves that state pretty well.

He got off to a rocky start, calling people names (e.g. his election opponents were "girlie-men") and trying to govern by force of initiative and personality.

But as USC law professor and syndicated columnist Susan Estrich said, "A funny thing happened on the way to his demise: He learned. He changed. He learned he had to make peace with the legislature, which means Democrats, if he was going to get anything done. And he wanted to get things done.

"So he buckled down," she said.

"He got rid of some of the rabid Republicans on his team, and if anyone is [angry] with him right now, it's the conservative Republicans who think he is too liberal, and a RINO – Republican In Name Only."

Schwarzenegger has been aggressive about California's many environmental worries, and he has tried to help schools. His appointees are generally strong, and while his presence is still large, he doesn't always lead with his macho personality.

If a muscle-bound guy like that can learn a thing or two, so can I.

Have I changed my tune about Ahhnold the Ham? He's doing much better, for sure he am.

SCOOT, SCOOTER

November 2005

The day Dick Cheney's aide Lewis "Scooter" Libby was indicted on five counts of lying to a grand jury thereby obstructing the court's ability to get to the truth of a national security leak, my dearly departed mother was right there in my head, speaking in my ear.

"Do not ... " she intoned. (The image was blurry so I don't know if she was wagging her finger, but probably.) "Do not derive pleasure from another person's misfortune."

Of course she is right. It's not nice, it's not attractive and it's certainly not charitable. So on occasions such as this when my adversaries are brought down, I have tried to temper my hootin' and hollerin'.

But the day U.S. Prosecutor Patrick Fitzgerald announced the indictment of Libby, my uncharitable glee overcame me. Rather than dredging up any more of Mother's Words to Live By, I called my dad for a different view.

He's past 90 and a tough Texan. He's spent all his adult life cavorting with similarly no-nonsense Texans in the Panhandle oilfields and in the Dallas and Houston offices of famously Republican and predictably conservative businessmen.

Until George W. Bush was elected president the first time, my dad was a registered Republican. But when Bush the Younger came on the scene, he shook his head and said, "I've never seen a man who could strut sittin' down," and that was that.

Bush hits my dad's wince button, as he does too many of us. Is it the arrogance? The silver spoon falling out of his mouth? The embarrassing military record? The inability to own up to error?

Is it the strut, the smirk, the swagger, the swindle? (By swindle, I mean the now-unmistakable massaging and manipulation of pre-war intelligence or, more to the point, lack of intelligence.)

Or is it the uneasy feeling, increasingly, that our emperor wears no clothes. Without his script-writers and play-makers, Cheney and Rove, Bush would simply be a joking, good ol' boy-style president, without maturity, depth or vision.

And what about these sidekicks — Cheney with his loyalists and cultivated news sources, Rove with his much-awed scorched earth politics? It may be this gang, even more than bungling Bush, who has moved people like my dad from dislike to disgust.

With no guts for telling the truth, with a lazy, egocentric press to let them get away with it, and a feeble opposition party to walk over, the Cheney-Rove-Bush administration took us into a falsely justified and dishonestly defended war. It has been a war of insurgency, not a fight for freedom, and we have lost more than 2,000 soldiers and hundreds of thousands of civilian lives.

They have deceptively, and somewhat successfully, tried to link the war against terror to the war in Iraq, when in fact that war seems to have added fuel to the fires of the terrorists. And they have, apparently, spent a lot of time in the cloak and dagger cover-up of all that trickery. Tell me, if you can, how that kind of incompetence and untruth is about freedom.

Libby is presumed innocent, although many say the case against him is a slam-dunk. (Excuse me, Mr. Tenet.) Maybe he didn't lie; maybe he won't go to jail; if he is found guilty, maybe he'll be pardoned. But his indictment, surely a chink in the Bush-Cheney-Rove armor, is a long-overdue first step at getting to the real puppet masters behind the curtain in the White house. And what I am glad about is not one man's indictment and possible punishment, but the revelation of the dishonest tactics and dirty tricks he and his bosses employ.

As my dad said, with not so much glee as sarcasm, "It couldn't happen to a nicer bunch."

Epilogue

The leak case involving Libby centered on the assertion in President Bush's January 2003, State of the Union address that Iraq had attempted to purchase material to build a nuclear weapon from the African country of Niger, citing this "fact" as one of several reasons to invade Iraq.

Ambassador Joseph Wilson, a 20-year career diplomat and former ambassador to Iraq, had previously traveled to Niger to investigate this allegation and reported no basis for it. But the statement showed up in the speech, anyway.

Wilson subsequently penned an article that appeared in the New York Times disputing the president's assertion and damaging the credibility of the White House's case for the war. In what many now believe was a retaliatory move against Wilson, Libby, then deputy to Vice President Dick Cheney, was dispatched to reveal to a reporter (actually several reporters) the identity of Wilson's wife, Valerie Plame, then an undercover agent for the CIA involved in the planning of Wilson's trip.

The brouhaha resulted in the appointment of Special Counselor Patrick Fitzgerald, a U.S attorney in Chicago, to get to the bottom of the leak. After much finger pointing, confusing testimony and failed memories, Fitzgerald's grand jury indicted Libby. His subsequent guilty verdict was followed with a 30-month sentence of imprisonment.

Yet, Libby, the highest-ranking government official convicted of a felony since the Iran-Contra affair, will not go to jail. President Bush, saying the sentence was excessive, promptly commuted Libby's sentence to two years of probation. He is required to pay a $250,000 fine to the federal government and can appeal his sentence. In fact, the president could still pardon him.

As it turns out, former Assistant Secretary of Defense Richard Armitage was the first leaker, mentioning Plame's name to columnist Richard Novak. But since Armitage did not mention, nor apparently did he know, Plame was undercover, he has not been prosecuted for the revelation. He is, however, being sued by the Wilsons along with …

Whoa. Let's take a deep breath. If you're confused reading this tale, think about how many legions of reporters have been confused trying to explain and write about it, this writer included. My apologies.

It's a story better explained by reading "Hubris: The Inside Story of Spin, Scandal and the Selling of the Iraq War," by Michael Isikoff and David Corn; or Jeffrey Toobin's careful reporting in The New Yorker or just about anything that comes up when you Google the names of any of the players. It's a hell of a tale, and I can't wait for the movie.

Karl Rove left the White House, but not the theatre, I'll bet. Wilson is talking about running for office, doncha know; Valerie has a book out; the current secretary of defense says he's not sure the war in Iraq was worth it; the former chair of the Federal Reserve Bank says the war is all about oil; the current general commanding the forces in Iraq says he doesn't know if the war in Iraq makes America safer; and, the Iraqis don't even know if they want us to go or stay.

The announced Democrat presidential candidates for 2008 each have a plan, sort of, for extricating the U.S. from the conflict, and the GOP candidates are looking for one. A majority of Americans no longer support the war, but the now Democrat-controlled Congress can't seem to muster its courage or will to get past the opposition party or the White House.

The conflict with Libby, Rove, Cheney and Wilson is far from over. Unfortunately, so is the loss of life in Iraq or the stubborn iron grip of the Bush administration.

Trying to bring a little perspective to this administration's ineptitude, I bought my dad a keychain with an LED read-out of the days, hours and minutes remaining until Bush is out of office. Some of his friends wanted one, too, so I called the store where I'd bought it in Washington, D.C. They would have to call me back, they said. They've been so popular, they're on back-order.

A MAN TO DO A WOMAN'S JOB

JUNE 2005

PROLOGUE

The first woman ever named to the U.S. Supreme Court, the thoughtful, dignified and fair-minded Justice Sandra Day O'Connor announced her retirement in 2005, setting up a contentious debate over her replacement. O'Connor served 24 terms on the high court and was often the "swing" or deciding vote on many cases.

ustice Sandra Day O'Connor seemed pretty happy about the choice of John G. Roberts Jr. to fill her slot on the U.S Supreme Court, except, as she astutely pointed out," he's not a woman."

So much for what a departing justice thinks. So much for what Laura Bush thinks. (She let it be known that she wanted a woman.)

In less than two decades, women finally found representation on the court, correcting several hundred years of not having a place there. But this president may undo all that. With the retirement of O'Connor, Justice Ruth Bader Ginsburg remains the sole woman on the top bench, and she is not well.

Maybe President Bush will appoint a woman the next time: He is likely to get another shot at this. But we can be pretty sure he will appoint someone to vote to overturn Roe v. Wade, the 1973 decision making first-term abortion legal. He probably already has, if you presume Roberts' writings to date.

Without question, Bush's commitment to a "culture of life" means his desire to overturn Roe. It is the key agenda item for his political handlers, the majority membership of the Senate and nearly every conservative organization in America. When some conservatives squawked Roberts might be too moderate, Bush's posse was quick to reassure them. If Roberts didn't take out Roe right away, he'd surely go after so-called partial birth abortion. Not to worry, they said. He won't disappoint like David Souter or Anthony Kennedy. And they are probably right.

Roberts' background, record, family life, credentials and judicial decisions will all be examined. But the tipping point will be abortion and whether women will continue to have the right to choose to have a legal and safe one. To believe otherwise is simply naïve.

To believe Bush is looking for a moderating influence – someone to heal the divisiveness on this issue – is foolhardy, as well. His actions speak otherwise.

I believe the president chose a man to do a woman's job on this court not because there weren't qualified women – he had plenty to choose from – but because he is building a court that looks like him. White, conservative men who will likely overturn Roe.

I'm going out on a limb here and predicting that unless some deep, dark, scandalous secret falls out of Roberts' closet, he will be confirmed. By all accounts, he's a nice guy and a super-smart lawyers' lawyer, with good Midwestern family values. Conservative but not crazy, they say. Religious but not rabid. Nor are the Democrats likely to find the grounds or the guts to oppose him successfully. And besides, the Democrats should save their fodder for the next likely-to-be-more-conservative choice.

But look where we are if Roberts is confirmed: Five men will decide whether to restrict a woman's right to legal abortion (or six if Bush gets another appointment.) The dissenters will be three or four – and only one of them will have ever been pregnant.

Bush clearly intends to push his anti-abortion agenda through his appointments to the court, in the Congress, on the stump, by hook or by crook. (And speaking of those, Karl Rove is plenty happy to give

Roberts the front page while he slinks out of the headlines and back into the safety of his boss' wide, protective net.)

"John Roberts is a mature legal intellectual, a fully developed conservative. That is the legacy this president intends to leave on the court," writes FOX News commentator, Susan Estrich.

"If he didn't appoint a woman or a minority to this seat, it is a pretty good indication that his first priority is to appoint young, extremely smart, extremely conservative judges, even if they happen to look very much like him, or maybe especially if they do, who have the capacity to change the court for decades to come."

Does this sound like FDR, the prototypical court-packer? Maybe, but Eleanor surely would have dissented.

Epilogue

Roberts was easily approved by the U.S. Senate and was sworn in as chief justice of the United States in Sept. 2005, though little was made of his well-known service to Bush. As an attorney, Roberts was called to Tallahasse, Fla., in 2000 to help the president's team of lawyers prepare their case in the vote recount controversy, advising this ad hoc team about ways to persuade the U. S. Supreme Court to take the case. That would have gotten my goat, but no one asked me.

In 2006, after the retirement of Chief Justice William Rehnquist, Bush got his chance to fill another slot, marking this court with another conservative, Samuel A. Alito, Jr. As a young attorney in the Eighties in the U.S. Deptartment of Justice, Alito sent a memo to his boss, the solicitor general, suggesting ways the Supreme Court could move toward an overturn of Roe. The justices had agreed to examine a Pennsylvania law restricting abortion, and Alito saw an opening there. According to Jeffrey Toobin, in his book "Nine: Inside the Secret World of the Supreme Court," Alito wrote, "What can be made of this opportunity to advance the goals of bringing about the eventual overruling of Roe v. Wade and, in the mean-

time, of mitigating its effects?" Not much doubt was left about Alito's opinion on abortion rights.

When two cases on late-term abortion (sometimes called partial-birth abortion) came before this new court in April 2007, the justices voted 5-to-4 to affirm the constitutionality of Congress' 2003 Partial Birth Abortion Ban Act, opening the door to the question of Roe's endurance wider.

Bush's new appointees to the bench wasted no time proving their anti-abortion credentials by joining Justices Antonin Scalia, Clarence Thomas and swing voter Anthony Kennedy in the narrow decision giving what Salon.com called "a gift card to his conservative constituency."

Justice Ruth Bader Ginsburg, the only woman left on the court, read her bitter dissent from the bench, saying the majority's opinion "cannot be understood as anything other than an effort to chip away a right declared again and again by this court, and with increasing comprehension of its centrality to women's lives." She called the ruling "alarming" and noted the conservative majority "tolerates, indeed applauds, federal intervention to ban nationwide a procedure found necessary and proper in certain cases" by doctor's groups, including gynecologists.

Ginsburg told an audience of women attorneys that while she and O'Connor did not agree on all issues, they shared certain experiences.

The high court may not have more than one justice who looks like you, she told them, but don't despair. There are lots of women in federal judgeships and they have nowhere to go but up.

HILLARY

November 2007

"Women were welcome to come in as workers but not as co-makers of the world."

> — EMILY BLAIR, Missouri suffragist
> and vice president of the National
> Democrat Party, 1924

O ver a cup of coffee and a lot of dish, my friend asked me if there was anything going on in the world I felt good about.

I surprised myself by answering without missing a beat. "We might elect a woman president of the United States!" I said.

She looked at me like I was crazy. Of course she knows that at this moment, in the early fall of 2007, Sen. Hillary Clinton, D-N.Y., and former first lady of the U.S., is poised to be the Democrat nominee for president in the 2008 elections.

Of course my friend knows I'm a Democrat. Of course she knows I'm also a skeptic, not as optimistic as I'd like to be about the future of the planet and the lives of the people on it.

An influential and accomplished civic leader in Oklahoma City, she is nevertheless alienated from the system and the process of electoral politics, groaning at the prospect of a rancorous 12-month election and the players in it.

So we were both a little taken aback at my absolute delight that Hillary might win the nomination and the presidency, both firsts for the U.S.

Indeed, for the last few months, Hillary — as she has now been branded — has led the pack of eight announced Democrats running for president in major polls and beats the ten announced Republicans as well, though at this writing, she just barely tops Rudy Giuliani. In spite of the uncertainties of Iowa and New Hampshire; a tiresome, yearlong election cycle; the systemic dysfunction of the Democratic Party; the virulent Anybody-but-Hillary crowd; and the unpredictability of the campaign trail, she might just win.

Imagine that, I said to myself, remembering a woman from Nevada named Maya Miller who ran for the U.S. Senate in 1972 but couldn't raise any money because no one thought a woman could win. Her situation inspired a group of young women in Washington, D.C., including me, to launch the Women's Campaign Fund to raise money for women in both parties running for office. When WCF started, there were 11 women in the U.S. Congress. Today, there are 90.

My enthusiasm for the election of women to public office goes way back. I remember standing in the convention hall in San Francisco in 1984 the night Geraldine Ferraro was chosen to run for vice president, the first woman ever on a national party ticket. National Public Radio correspondent, Linda Wertheimer, began her lead-in the next day on "All Things Considered" with these words: "It's a girl!"

I remember former U.S. House member, Patricia Schroeder, D-Colo., bringing her two small children with her to her office at the U.S. Capitol when she chaired the House Armed Services Committee. They crawled around under her desk waiting for her to return.

I remember working to help elect big, brassy Bella Abzug, D-N.Y., with her floppy hats and over-stuffed briefcase; Madeleine Kunin, the dignified governor of Vermont; Millicent Fenwick, R-N.J., who smoked a pipe and took cash donations from women in her district who were concerned their husbands would otherwise notice them supporting a woman.

I remember raising money for Elizabeth Holtzman, D-N.Y., a tough criminal prosecutor who wore white, wrist-length gloves and carried her little pocketbook to the podium at every campaign appearance;

and Barbara Jordan, D-Texas, one of the most eloquent public servants this country has had.

I remember the first woman to serve in the U.S. Congress was Jeanette Rankin, D-Mont., elected in 1917, two years before women could even vote. Rankin famously said, "You can no more win a war, than you can win an earthquake." I remember the first female member of Congress from Oklahoma was Alice Robertson elected in 1922, and Oklahoma didn't send another woman for 84 years, when Mary Fallin, R-Okla. City, was elected in 2006.

I applauded Ann Richards' election as governor of Texas; Shirley Chisholm's strength as the first black woman in Congress; and the victory of Nancy Pelosi, D-Calif., as first woman speaker of the U.S. House.

I have spent much so much of my professional life helping women get elected to public office; it's a natural thing for me to land in the Hillary camp. Yet it is more than her womanhood I support.

I think she brings to the job many things America needs in a president today. She is smart and competent, and we are long overdue for both. She is committed to public service, is hardworking and increasingly demonstrates a command of the issues and trials facing the nation and the world.

Uniquely, as a woman, she brings the wisdom of a mother; the understanding of a daughter; the loyalty of a wife and partner; the lessons of juggling family and work, and the sensibilities of more than half the population of the country.

Certainly, she is not without faults — I wish she'd seen the futility of this war in Iraq and voted against it; I wish she'd relax more; I wish she'd come up with clear, short answers and not long, drawn-out dodges; and I wish she didn't draw the ire of so many Republicans.

Her detractors are many. They are women like her — successful, well-educated contemporaries — who are uneasy about her. Are they jealous? Mistrustful? Not ready themselves, so how could she be? Or they are women unlike her who cannot understand her certainty and toughness. They are women and men who think she can't win a general election and fear her defeat would mean four more years of ineffective leadership. There are those who want her in the White House because they want Bill there, too. There are those who oppose her because she didn't leave Bill, and those who support her because she didn't leave Bill.

She got where she is because of her husband! Some cry. She got where she is in spite of her husband, say others.

She's too liberal; she won't tell us where she stands. She's too calculating, cold, yet she's got cleavage and she's playing the woman card. She handles herself with composure and dignity, but she's too scripted and programmed.

OK. Not everybody's right for every job. For example, I'd love to hear the quick and elegant Barack Obama take on Rush Limbaugh, and John Edwards would be brilliant as Hamlet or arguing before the Supreme Court. But neither of these men is tough or hungry enough, in my view, to go the distance. Bill Richardson seems to know how to negotiate with foreign dictators, so give him a cabinet post. Chris Dodd and Joe Biden are effective in the U.S. Senate, so let them stay there. And Dennis Kucinich? Every party needs its gadfly.

As for the other team, John McCain is the country's most credible military statesman, but I don't think he has the temperament to lead a diverse nation. Mitt Romney can run a business, but talk about cold . . . And Rudy Giuliani, well, he's quite The Operator, turning every sow's ear into a silk purse all behind a magician's cape. If he can get over himself, he could make a bundle lobbying.

So back to Hillary. I like it that the other candidates take themselves too seriously to let us call them "Mitt" or "John," yet this supposedly uptight woman is fine with the casual moniker, Hillary. I like it that she's been pregnant like me; that's she had some bad days in her marriage, like me; that she's raised a child, like me; that she's worried about women and children and their health care, like me; and that she ran out of patience for the Bush administration long ago, also like me.

Win or lose, the real possibility of a woman president is ground-breaking. In 1978, I remember telling a national gathering of women that we had an "old boys' network" and what we needed was an "old girls' network." Now, I am proud to say, we've got one. Let's use it.

SEVEN

RIGHTS VS. MIGHT

CHOOSING LIFE

APRIL 1999

Seven a.m. on my daughter's 16th birthday, and I am sitting in a state patrol test center while she takes her driver's test for the much-anticipated license to freedom. Tonight, we plan to go to her favorite local restaurant and on the weekend, we'll have some of her friends over for hamburgers and gooey ice cream and cake in the back yard.

She's happy. She's loved. She's alive. She is lucky to be all of those things, and she is just beginning to know it.

Kids who have come into this test center to get their licenses are actually galloping. A license! Maybe a car! No more begging rides from Mom and Dad. A ticket to ride, and life is looking up.

I sit here, watching and smiling, knowing these happy, goofy kids can't possibly realize yet what a hassle car payments and repairs and traffic and tickets and maybe car accidents are going to be. They can't imagine a mother's anxiety as her daughter is turned loose behind the wheel of a machine capable of destruction, or a father's worry as she now spends hours away from home, on her own.

There is so much my daughter cannot know yet. So much joy and satisfaction waiting for her, but so much sadness and despair, too. Lots of decisions for her to make, lots of choices about the way she will make them and how she will live her life.

David Packman, the rabbi from my congregation, Temple B'nai Israel in Oklahoma City, talks about these choices in Freudian and in biblical terms, first explaining "libido" – our creative, productive, joyfully alive side – and "thanatos" (Greek for death), our destructive, dark and evil side.

"We have both," said Packman.

"As parents, our job is to try to strengthen libido and undercut the power of thanatos. We can't always stop it, that impulse to destroy, but we must be vigilant."

Yesterday, when my daughter was still 15, I watched the events at Columbine High School in Littleton, Colo., stunned, then angry, then heartsick. Still today, our heads spin with disbelief about these terrible murders, the boys who caused them, the kids who taunted those boys, the parents who raised those boys, the images that attracted and entertained them.

I am dragged down by despair, confused and frightened by this. If I can't understand, how can a 16-year-old bouncing around in Converse tennis shoes and cut-offs?

"These kids," said the rabbi, speaking of the perpetrators of the Colorado murders, "were attracted to the 'thanatos' of life, represented by Hitler, by the color black, by destructives games … their parents didn't necessarily cause it, but we cannot allow it.

"Suicide is the death of libido and the triumph of thanatos," he told me. "We have all known at least moments of that depression and despair. But we have to beat it back or simply get through it."

On days like yesterday when 14 kids and one adult were killed by someone else's "thanatos," when my own soft-eyed child is trying to grow up in a world gone nearly mad, it's not easy to beat it back. While she skips with carefree optimism around the corner of adolescence, I know what dangers lie on the other side.

Sometimes I ask myself: In the face of this horror, what does she want with this freedom? Why try to do well or be good? Why go to school? Why even go out the front door? Why teach them to struggle against hate when a classmate is teasing, taunting, torturing? Why teach them to resist fear when classmates have guns? Really; why bother?

In a world where this week's violence tops last, where children viciously end each other's lives and then their own, where signs of sadness and hatred were all around but parents seem not to have noticed, I have to help her choose hope and choose life. For her, for now, it's as simple as a driver's license and a birthday party. But for me, I have to dig deeper.

The rabbi also reminded me of one of Judaism's strongest tenets, one that speaks to our source of deep-down, ages-old optimism. (For attribution, this is God speaking in Deuteronomy, read at Yom Kippur, the Day of Atonement.)

" ... I have set before you today, life and prosperity, death and adversity ... choose life so that you and your descendants may live."

MAKE ABORTION AVAILABLE
JANUARY 1998

n 1963 — my junior year in high school and a full decade before Roe v. Wade was decided — my mother handed me a newspaper article about a teen-age girl in our home town who died trying to end her unwanted pregnancy by inserting a pair of scissors into her own womb.

"Please, please," my mother said. "Come to me if you're ever in trouble like this. I promise I will help."

How lucky I was to have a mother who, in spite of abortion's illegality, had the courage to talk about it and to let me know she would stand up for me in spite of the taboo surrounding it. But while she was offering invaluable support, she was promising something she probably couldn't have given me then or now, even after 25 years of legal abortion. Today my right to a safe abortion is certainly legal, but it is a right that is almost impossible to exercise.

In the Fifties and Sixties, the number of illegal abortions performed in the United States may have been as high as 1.2 million, including 5,000 deaths annually. Before Roe, untrained or unethical medical workers, friends, husbands and boyfriends of pregnant women or women themselves tried to end their pregnancies using dangerous methods like throwing themselves down stairs, drinking Drano, douching with Lysol or inserting objects into their wombs like an umbrella, plastic tubing, a garden hose or the now infamous coat hanger.

By making abortion legal in Roe, the U.S. Supreme Court did not invent the surgical procedure. But since Roe, abortions are very safe. In 1991, there were only 11 known deaths in the entire United States from almost 1.5 million legal abortions.

The U.S. Supreme Court's decision in Roe was arguably the most important day for the health and safety of women in my lifetime. With Roe, women could make the decision to end dangerous or unsupportable pregnancies within the privacy of their own homes, doctor's offices and consciences. And doctors were finally free to perform those procedures safely and legally, without fear of legal reprisal.

So what's the problem? The most conservative court in 50 years has embraced and reaffirmed Roe; poll after poll shows that a huge majority of Americans want to keep abortion safe and legal; and for eight years, we have had a president, Bill Clinton – the first since Roe was decided – willing to take a strong stand for abortion rights.

But make no mistake about it: In the trenches, where it counts, in clinics and doctor's offices, the radical anti-abortion right is winning. Abortion may be legal, but can you get one? Not easily. At the crux of the matter is a question asked by writer Jack Hitt.

"Can people be said to possess a right if they're too afraid to exercise it?"

Through intimidation, fear, financial threats, clinic bombings, violence and even murder, anti-abortion fanatics have driven away all but a few abortion providers. In two clinics and just a handful of offices in central Oklahoma, there are only a few physicians who will still perform abortions and only 2,000 left in the entire United States.

Today, Planned Parenthood of Central Oklahoma can refer patients to only three reputable physicians in the state for a safe abortion. It is virtually impossible to get a first-trimester abortion in any hospital in the area. And while there may be individual physicians willing to perform procedures on some of their private patients, they won't talk about it.

Of those 2,000 doctors who will perform abortions, nearly 59 percent are 65 or older. For them, abortion is not about politics or morality; it's about safety. They were in medicine before Roe, when young women arrived at hospitals near death from self-induced abortions. Their initial encounter with abortion was not as a political argument or an agenda item in an HMO liability committee meeting, but as an emergency. These doctors go on providing abortions because they know they are saving lives.

"I respect these people who have picketed outside my office for 25 years," one doctor told The New York Times.

"But I know what would happen if they were successful politically — a lot more tragedy, a lot more deaths. We have saved ... hundreds of thousands of lives."

These courageous practitioners do their work in a kind of "medical shadowland," where doctors wear bullet-proof vests, and security guards patrol their clinics, and sometimes their homes, 24 hours a day.

Today's medical community of frightened physicians, medical school and hospital administrators, mostly unfamiliar with the horrors of illegal or unavailable abortion, is reacting, in part, to the argument that abortion is immoral; they are bowing to financial and political pressure. They don't even teach abortion procedures in medical schools anymore. As one local gynecologist told me, "They're chickens."

It's understandable. If your practice — indeed, your own safety and that of your family, your patients and employees — is at risk, it's understandable that you might be unwilling to perform abortions. Let someone else do it, you say. Let residents get their own training. Let patients go elsewhere. Not in our emergency room. Not in our hospital. It's understandable, but not acceptable.

What are frightened women and girls to do? What if you live in Ardmore, Okla.? There are no providers there. Can you afford the time and money to travel here or to Dallas? What if you wait for your Medicaid check and by then, it's your second trimester? You certainly can't afford an abortion now.

I offer a challenge to the medical community. While it may no longer be possible to mandate medical training for abortion, administrators and faculty can make it easier for those who want the training by offering a curriculum that teaches safe abortion as an option and a response to the need for indigent care. It is a legal option for patients and should be one physicians can offer them. I challenge you, too, to use your collective power as physicians before hospital and HMO committees, before anti-abortion groups and with law enforcement to provide women a safe, medical option they are entitled to have.

It is daunting, but it is still possible to get an abortion in Oklahoma, and women are not yet taking extreme measures to end their pregnancies. But will they, when they can no longer find a doctor to provide one? Will they when they cannot drive to another state or country? Who will help our daughters and their daughters when this generation of doctors that "still remembers" isn't around, but hasn't been replaced because no one knows how to do their work or has the courage to try?

Epilogue

Since this column was published, there has been good news and bad for women who want safe and legal abortion.

In October 2000, the U.S. Food and Drug Administration finally approved the use of RU-486 in the United States, an oral abortifacient (medically induced abortion) already available to women for many years in Europe. Supervised by a physician, the series of three similar medications is given to a pregnant woman at several week intervals prior to seven weeks of pregnancy. It is not inexpensive, so poor women continue to be deprived of this option. But it is safe, private, and now, legal. Doctors who, for whatever reasons, do not perform surgical abortions are increasingly willing to prescribe RU-486.

But accessibility to surgical abortion remains a growing problem, and abortion opponents using violent tactics are largely to blame. In 1999, Dr. Barnett Slepian, a private practitioner in upstate New York and the father of young children, was murdered in his home by anti-abortion advocates who proudly claimed the action in the name of what they call their holy war. Another serious threat to accessibility to safe and legal abortion are religious-based hospitals that require doctors and medical personnel to pledge not to perform the procedure in their facility.

Roe, itself, has been threatened and could be overturned, as it hangs in the U.S. Supreme Court by a margin of one or two votes on most cases. With the election of George W. Bush as president, and hints by several Court justices of retirement, the right to safe and legal abortion is threatened again. It is an issue the American people consistently believe should be left up to women and their families and an issue the Congress and state legislatures continue to use to stack up political points.

POSTSCRIPT

While still-legal abortions may be harder and harder to get, contraception should be easier.

After clear evidence that emergency contraception (also known as Plan B or the morning after pill) was safe for women over the counter, the Bush-appointed commissioners on the Food and Drug Administration refused to approve it . The medicine had been available by prescription for some years, and is a safe, simple, inexpensive pill that young women were "improvising" anyway.

One young woman told me how it works for her and her friends: "I take birth control pills, but if I forget or think for any reason I might have gotten pregnant, you know, 'last night,' I just take a handful of birth control pills and it works the same way. That's what all my friends do."

Where there's a will there's a way, and the Bush administration was naively, stubbornly and patronizingly denying a perfectly good option to women, as well as ignoring the science behind it. So the women in the U.S. Senate – specifically, Sen. Hillary Clinton, D-N.Y. and Sen. Barbara Boxer, D-Calif. – held up Bush's appointment to the FDA until he gave the contraception the green light. An example, I think, of women's power politics working for women.

But while contraception may be easier to get, abortion is not. The National Abortion Foundation reports that violence toward abortion providers has killed seven people, including three doctors, two clinic employ-

ees, a security guard and a clinic escort. Since 1977 in the U.S. and Canada crimes against abortion providers have included 41 bombings, 173 arsons and 619 bomb threats. The most recent event was in May 2007, when an unidentified person deliberately set fire to a Planned Parenthood clinic in Virginia Beach, Va.

Planned Parenthood of Central Oklahoma does not provide abortions in its clinics, and today it refers its patients to only two doctors in the state.

COMMON GROUND
MARCH 2006

Since January 1973, when the U.S. Supreme Court decided abortion was legal in the first trimester of pregnancy, there has been a war-like conflict in America between those who believe a woman should make her own decisions about reproduction and those who believe abortion is murder and should be banned.

In the ensuing years since Roe v. Wade was decided, Americans have become increasingly at odds about this issue, with no success at reaching compromise. Frankly, there has been little effort on either side to try.

Today, most Americans – including most Oklahomans – still believe that abortion should remain safe and legal, but more passionate opponents of the procedure hold the power cards, controlling the federal branch of government, the U.S. Congress, many state legislatures, and possibly the U.S. Supreme Court.

Warriors in this battle divide into three categories: the aggressive, go-for-broke Front-Line Combatants, like the legislators in the state of South Dakota that recently banned abortion hoping the U.S. Supreme Court will uphold that decision and overturn Roe; the Snipers, such as Oklahoma's state Rep. Thad Balkman, D-Norman, who is sponsoring legislation limiting access to contraception and thereby chipping away at both the right to an abortion and the possibility of preventing them; and the Stunned Onlookers – those of us who are frozen in inaction by the onslaught of these two armies and the sense that we can't win.

In Oklahoma – and here I hope to motivate Stunned Onlookers into action – we are closer to South Dakota than we realize.

Quietly lying dormant in Title 21, Sec. 861 of the Oklahoma Statutes is a ban on abortion unless a woman's life is in danger. If Roe were overturned, that statute, currently unconstitutional, would be resurrected. Front-line combat without even a stop at the courthouse.

Snipers are busy in Oklahoma, too, chipping away at legal abortion by passing restriction after restriction — parental consent measures, forced physician and patient registration requirements, required conversation between doctor and patient about purported fetal pain, etc.

Is it too late to find common ground? Can we talk or compromise our way out of this warring quagmire?

Reasonable people on both sides will say preventing abortion and preventing unwanted pregnancies are the common ground. Together, we have to put ideologies aside and put women's health first. Here's a start:

- Contraception has to be the starting point. Without it, we will have chaos. Emergency contraception and new contraception technologies should be easily accessible and available. Recently Wal-Mart's pharmacies, responding to their female customers who demanded this protection, began to stock EC (the morning-after pill) and told their pharmacists to fill prescriptions for it.

- Pharmacists should be encouraged to fill any and all doctors' prescriptions for legal contraception and should not be excused for refusing to do so. Pharmacists have a duty to dispense medication, not moral judgment. At a minimum, objecting pharmacists and doctors should be required to refer patients to other, cooperating professionals.

- Pregnancy prevention programs for teens must be taken seriously. Abstinence programs are valuable, but abstinence ONLY programs fail. Just ask the folks at Planned Parenthood of Tulsa who were called in to rescue one nearby rural school district where an abstinence-only program resulted in an outbreak of epidemic gonorrhea. Teens are not stupid. They need to understand the consequences of unintended pregnancies and taught how to avoid them. Keeping them stupid and barefoot, as the old saying goes, surely does just keep them pregnant.

- The government should not force women to carry pregnancies to term, especially those women who have been raped, victimized by incest or whose life or health would be endangered. Any legislation that does not include those exceptions should be defeated.

- Equity in insurance coverage should be pushed; if your insurance policy covers Viagra, it ought to cover contraception too.

I asked Balkman if he thought there was common ground to be found on this issue. After thinking about it for a while, he said, "We in the pro-life movement have found common ground by taking this decision out of the hands of the federal government and putting it into the hands of the states."

But not, I asked, into the hands of women and their families? No, he said.

"Back to the states."

Epilogue

Rep. Balkman was defeated in the 2006 elections, but efforts to make abortion illegal continue vigorously without him.

In Oklahoma, the 2006 state Legislature passed a measure that required physicians to narrow their definition of "medical emergency," prohibited them from counseling patients to terminate pregnancies even if they believed the patient's or baby's health were endangered, and restricted access to abortion on several other fronts. Troubled by the Legislature's meddling between doctors and their patients, Gov. Brad Henry vetoed the bill. The Legislature then added exceptions for victims of rape or incest, but left most of the bill intact. The revised bill passed easily, and is now law in Oklahoma.

Several "pregnancy prevention" bills – measures one would think would put all of us on common ground – were introduced and got nowhere but could be introduced in 2008. One of those bills allows access to legal, traditional contraception and more advanced emergency contraception; one requires "compassionate care" for victims of rape; and another insists on medically accurate information in sex education classes.

In the meantime, the U.S. Supreme Court took its first serious swipe at legal abortion since Roe v. Wade was decided in 1973.

A lower court ban on a medical procedure called late-term (or partial-birth) abortion was narrowly upheld by a 5-to-4 decision in 2006. The court is now poised to hear and decide more cases restricting legal abortion, a clear goal of the George W. Bush administration and one he seems to be accomplishing.

Yet most Americans, including most Oklahomans, do not want abortion to become illegal. The Tulsa World conducted a poll in April 2007, of likely Oklahoma voters, 75 percent of whom still believe abortion should be a medical decision involving a woman and her doctor.

There is also public support for contraception and sex education – in other words, information and the means to prevent pregnancies – but these attitudes don't seem to translate into legislative action.

Abortion-rights activists continue to regroup and re-energize to defeat measures like the one proposed in South Dakota in 2006. (See above) There the state Legislature proposed a ban on all abortions making exception only for the endangered life of the mother, but not excepting victims of rape or incest or in cases of the threatened health of the mother. Voters in South Dakota, where there is only one clinic performing abortions, gathered enough signatures on a petition and took the question to the voters who defeated the ban with a resounding majority. Even those opposed to abortions in some circumstances (such as late-term abortion) believed the South Dakota measure lacked compassion and went too far.

Common ground may exist in Oklahoma and elsewhere in the country, but the will to reach it, and the political courage to fight for it, currently does not.

REPUBLICANS FOR CHOICE

September 2005

o understand the divisiveness of the abortion issue in purely partisan political terms, one has to look no further than the written platforms of each national party.

Lengthy documents for both Democrats and Republicans, these statements of principle are an informative way to see in writing what each party's leaders and key policy-makers believe. Individual candidates may choose to ignore these planks, but they are, nevertheless, the "ultimate source" for a party's standards. The documents offer predictably different perspectives on tax increases, health care, etc.

But in no other area is there such disparity than in each party's position on abortion. They are entirely opposite.

In the national Republican Party Platform there is a full page dedicated to opposition to abortion, supporting a "human life amendment" to the U.S. Constitution; opposing giving information on birth control to minors without parental consent, and on and on.

In the Democrats' national platform, there is just one paragraph saying the party "stands proudly for a woman's right to choose, consistent with Roe v. Wade and regardless of her ability to pay." "Abortion," the Democrats' platform reads, "should be safe, legal and rare."

If you are a Republican supporting abortion rights in America today — and there are a lot of you quietly hiding out there — you've been shoved into a closet by your leaders. It's time for you to shove back.

While the majority of Americans, including a majority of Republicans, still believe abortion should be safe and legal, and that Roe should not be overturned, those views are not being reflected by legislators writing laws or casting votes for us. In other words, the moderates in the GOP – and there are many both nationally and here in Oklahoma – have been silenced since 1980 when, according to Ann E.W. Stone, National Chair of Republicans for Choice (RFC), the party "was hijacked by a band of dedicated and vocal anti-choice fanatics."

There's not much doubt about that, though some may wince at the use of the word "fanatics" to describe those opposed to abortion. But the extreme policies of national and some statewide GOPs leave little room for moderates on both sides of this issue to find common ground.

The anti-abortion Republicans currently control the White House, both houses of Congress, the Oklahoma state House and possibly next year, our state Senate. So a rank-and-file business-oriented, fiscally-conservative, tax-cutting GOP who may also believe a woman's decisions about reproduction should be her own private choice, have a tough row to hoe. Or they can give up on abortion rights in the Republican Party, which seems to have happened.

Yet there are organizations within the GOP working to make room in the party for abortion-rights moderates. RFC, a political action committee founded in 1990, operates on the principle that abortion is not only a divisive issue in America; it is a dangerous one for the Republican Party. Women left the party over this issue in the first Clinton election and only came back to Bush because of national security. RFC hopes to eliminate the human life amendment plank from the GOP platform.

A list of GOP-majority organizations includes the Women's Reproductive Rights Assistance Project which helps poor women fund a safe abortion; My Party Too, which advocates for traditional Republican principles of individual responsibility and personal freedom; and the Republican Youth Majority, a national network of fiscally conservative college students and young professionals who are training new leadership for the Republican Party and support abortion rights.

Decisions about reproduction ought not to be considered Democrat or Republican, liberal or conservative or political at all. Unfortunately they are, and today, all eyes are on the GOP to stand up for those personal freedoms or let the rest of us down. The party has made it tougher, but not impossible, to support abortion rights. So to all moderate, fair-minded Republicans out there: Come out, come out, wherever you are, and stand proudly as a Republican for choice.

Epilogue

Preserving legal abortion remains an uphill battle, especially for Republicans, with the President and vocal members of the GOP opposing it. And while the majority of the U.S. House and Senate is now Democrat, it's a slim majority. The focus for legal abortion is in the courts, White House and state legislatures, currently, with the White House holding the most cards. Yet a July 2007 poll conducted by the firm Fabrizio, McLaughlin & Associates and co-sponsored by the Republican Majority for Choice (RMC) found that 72 percent of self-proclaimed Republicans believe the government should not play a role in controlling choices for women, "believing instead that the decision to have an abortion should lie with women, their doctors, and their families."

As for the presidential election of 2008, the only GOP candidate who offers his party a position supporting abortion rights is former NYC Mayor, Rudy Giuliani.

One visible and well-funded abortion rights organization affiliated with the Republican Party is RMC. Its board, staff, advisory committee and fundraisers include some of the most respected names in Republican Party politics, then and now, including Mrs. Barry Goldwater, former U.S. senators Nancy Kassebaum, R-Kan., and Alan Simpson, R-Wyo., four or five U.S. Senators, a dozen U.S. House Members, former Governors Pete Wilson, Calif., and Christine Todd Whitman, N.J.

From the RMC website, "As former Senator Fred Thompson prepares to announce his candidacy to join Mitt Romney and John McCain, among

others, as anti-choice candidates, they should be reminded that the major-
ity of the Party believes the GOP has spent too much time focusing on
moral issues such as abortion and gay marriage," said Jennifer Stockman,
RMC co-chair.

"The presidential candidates need to acknowledge that there is an
overwhelming majority of Republicans – real Republicans – who are
frustrated with the rampant pandering to the far-right minority that has
only resulted in a hostile social agenda that divides the Party and the
country."

RESCUING THE EVIDENCE

AUGUST 2005

"Human history becomes more and more a race between education and catastrophy."

— H.G. WELLS, 1921

istorians believe that approximately 11 million people perished in the Nazi Holocaust of World War II, and based on documents and registries, they estimate at least 180,000 survived.

There surely are other survivors the world doesn't know about: those who could not tell their stories; children who never knew the full saga of their parentage; children and adults who were rescued, changed their identities and remained "in hiding," not speaking of or even knowing their histories.

Relatively few survivors are alive today. And every day, more and more of these witnesses — survivors, liberators, rescuers, refugees, bystanders — die. Within the next decade, the world will lose nearly all of its eyewitnesses to one of history's darkest eras.

With the loss of those first-hand accounts, we will also lose the power of a personally told history.

Now historians, archivists and the family members of survivors are in an urgent race, to find, research and record these stories in an effort the U.S. Holocaust Memorial Museum calls "Rescuing the Evidence."

The children and grandchildren of survivors and liberators are combing museum Web sites and survivor registries to find tracings of lost family members.

Filmmakers are making oral and visual histories, the closest thing to a first-person account. Families have stepped up to help in the race to gather history. One family donated photographs found in a box in a

New Jersey attic, another copied documents from a great-uncle's papers in Poland, yet another studied the papers of a murdered German physician bought by a Tulsa man on eBay.

Conservationists are preserving diaries from England and savings bits of fabric from blankets, yellow stars, ragged pink triangles, prison uniforms and a wedding dress made of the parachute material of a fallen soldier, all from the death camps.

War veterans are dredging up tales and memorabilia of that time.

Children and grandchildren of victims and survivors are rescuing all manner of things that bespeak their family's memories – horrible and cherished – establishing proof that these atrocities certainly did happen.

Lest we doubt. Lest we deny. Lest we allow it to happen again. If humankind has any hope of preventing this kind of catastrophe we must begin by learning what happened before.

One opportunity to learn will be through two exhibitions in downtown Oklahoma City, Sept. 15–Oct. 23, at Untitled [ArtSpace] 1 N.E. 3rd St.

"Nazi Persecution of Homosexuals 1933-1945" is a traveling exhibition of the U.S. Holocaust Memorial Museum. Few people know gay men were persecuted and murdered by the Nazi regime; this brilliant exhibition traces that history in photographs and documents.

"Rescuers: Portraits of Moral Courage," is a collection of photographs and interviews of Europeans who risked their lives to rescue Jews targeted for persecution. Both exhibitions can be seen with printed material and trained docents (guides) to help visitors understand.

Understand? Is it possible to understand this kind of horror? Is it possible to understand the social and cultural forces that allowed millions to sit by and watch as their neighbors – Jewish, Gypsy, homosexual, disabled, etc. – were arrested, imprisoned or shot before their eyes? Is it possible to understand how some remained bystanders but others found the courage to be rescuers and saviors?

These acts seem as impossible to understand as the acts of hatred and terrorism that stalk us now. But this isn't even ancient history. The prisoners at Auschwitz were liberated just 60 years ago; that's modern history, our history. History our parents and grandparents can tell us about.

Manya and Meyer Korenblit live in Ponca City, Okla., but were born in Poland in the 1920s. Liberated by the Americans and Russians in 1945, each is a survivor of multiple imprisonments in concentration and forced labor camps, including Auschwitz-Birkenau and Dachau. In their book, "Until We Meet Again," their son Michael Korenblit of Edmond, Okla., writes of a Jewish expression taught to him by his parents. It is what he has taught his children and the reason, he says, he and the children of other survivors must teach their histories.

"When you help save one person, it is as though you have saved the world."

Epilogue

More than 5,000 people saw the two exhibitions in downtown Oklahoma City and learned about some of the homosexual victims as well as some of the rescuers in the Nazi Holocaust. Since then, Oklahoma has lost more of its own citizens who were Holocaust survivors.

Oklahoma City's Jewish Federation has taken seriously the task of preserving the memory, dignity and histories of those lost and those who survived in an annual Yom HaShoah (Holocaust remembrance) ceremony each April.

Worldwide, more information is uncovered, and more evidence is rescued daily.

In 2006, an agreement was finally reached for the release of millions of documents and files stored but locked away since the end of World War II at the International Tracing Service (ITS) in Bad Arolsen, Germany. The U.S. Holocaust Memorial Museum in Washington, D.C, led the years-long effort to persuade 11 nations to alter international treaties and obtain the release of these records from warehouses full of papers, files and photographs from ITS – records kept by the Nazis themselves.

In August 2007, the Holocaust Museum and Yad Vashem, the memorial to the Holocaust in Jerusalem, received the first shipments of archival materials of the approximately 13.5 million pages of deportation files, arrest records and ghetto and concentration camp documentation from ITS. Future transfers will include the ITS Central Name Index including millions of pages of forced and slave labor records, and displaced persons camp and resettlement records. Survivors and their families will be able to trace the history of their own imprisonment, and the descendants of those who died can learn more about how, when and where the killings occurred.

The widespread appeal has been effective, including a recent example of a survivor who lives here in Oklahoma.

Helga Paige came to the Jewish Federation from her home in Enid, Okla., in late 2005 to talk to someone about her own history. Helga (Cerajewski) Paige was only 21-days old when she was liberated by the U.S. 45th Infantry Division from Dachau, a large concentration camp outside Munich, Germany. From Dachau, Helga was taken to a nearby hospital, treated for typhoid and sent to an orphanage in Munich. She does not know how she got there, but she remained there until she was six, when her mother came for her.

Before World War II, Helga's mother, a Polish woman, owned a guesthouse with her then-husband in Munich. When the Nazis came to power in Germany, the couple denounced the party in general and Hitler, in particular. They were arrested for this dissent and sent, over time, to three concentration camps, first to Bergen-Belsen, then to Auschwitz – both in Poland – then to Dachau.

Some years later, she told Helga the circumstances of her birth. In a dark corner of one of Dachau's barracks, Helga's mother was raped and became pregnant by a German SS guard, and gave birth to Helga in the *barracks. Soon after, Soviet soldiers liberated Dachau; Helga's mother left the camp, and the infant Helga, was taken away.*

With her mother and her new husband, an American military officer, Helga eventually made her way to the U.S. and to Enid, Okla., where she lives today. Helga told her story – one never told outside her immediate family – at the Oklahoma City Jewish Federation's Holocaust Remembrance Day event in the spring of 2006.

The challenge of Holocaust remembrance – indeed, a most powerful way to retell and learn from history – is to record it, and to record it in the first-person account, if possible, from institutions and individuals before it is lost forever.

FREE SPEECH AND FLAGPOLES

AUGUST 2001

PROLOGUE

In the spring of 2001, the Cimarron Alliance Foundation of Oklahoma, an education and advocacy group for gays and lesbians in Oklahoma City, "rented" 44 city light poles on the gay pride parade route (primarily along Classen Blvd.) to display banners with the group's symbol. For years, the city had rented these poles as well as bus stop benches to civic organizations to announce upcoming or ongoing events.

aper work done. Fee paid by Cimarron. Up went the banners.

The mayor of Oklahoma City Kirk Humphreys, believed the gay pride message was "negative" for the city and ordered the banners taken down.

Cimarron said, publicly, they considered the removal a discriminatory act and a violation of the group's constitutional right to free speech. The city attorney, concerned the city might indeed be vulnerable to legal action, advised the mayor to put the banners back up, and the mayor complied.

But Humphreys was clearly galled. Personally offended by homosexuality, he said any advertising of gay and lesbian groups or events was bad for the city and led the Oklahoma City Council to adopt a new, more restrictive policy (see below).

During the relatively short but heated controversy, bus stop benches that sported Cimarron's symbol were damaged with anti-gay messages, and Oklahoma City sported a big, embarrassing black eye in local and regional press accounts.

A few days after Humphreys fired the first shot in what has now become known as the "banner policy flap," a dozen or so bus stop benches in Oklahoma City were vandalized.

The Cimarron Alliance had used the backs of those benches to communicate its members' pride, paying for the ad space by following city procedures.

After the mayor's remarks suggesting Cimarron's message was not a positive one for the city, graffiti was spray-painted on bus benches over Cimarron's message.

It wasn't the nastiest graffiti you've ever seen — even homophobic Oklahomans are restrained — but the point was made. Citing Bible verses and using the word "straight," it was clear that overnight, anti-gay sentiments, harsher even than the mayor's, had been expressed via the destruction of city property, and in a way clearly meant to display hostility toward homosexuals.

Following these graffiti episodes, the mayor issued a statement decrying the vandalism. But few people knew about the statement against the vandalism, thanks to what I will generously call a lazy press corps — and in this case, that includes the Oklahoma Gazette. Only radio station KTOK-AM and television station KFOR picked up on his statement.

In written remarks, Humphreys said, " ... Vandalizing city property is a crime. The public discussion about city banner policies and the criminal spray painting of messages are very different matters.

"Our community will not tolerate violence directed at any of our citizens regardless of race, color, religion, age, gender, sexual preference, disability or any other distinction ... The city manager shares my concern about this incident and has assured me that there will be a full and complete investigation."

If you didn't know the mayor had distributed this statement to all Oklahoma City media outlets, you wouldn't realize he at least understands his responsibility to protect all citizens and all property of this community from violence — even if those citizens are gay or the property they utilize carries a message from the gay community. The mayor should get credit for that.

Yet this week the majority of Oklahoma City Council members (with Amy Brooks, Willa Johnson and Ann Simank dissenting), led by the mayor, voted to adopt a new policy that will prohibit banners or bus stops from bearing religious or social advocacy messages, with that determination left up to the city manager's office. In the years the mayor has been in office, he has not objected to any banners or bus stop ads, and more than thousands have been hoisted. He may not have liked them, but he didn't make it a public issue.

But now, instigated by his distaste for the Cimarron Alliance banners, down they all come, and up goes a policy that particular city property cannot be used for speaking freely. For me, there are more than a few problems with this.

First, the new Oklahoma City ordinance is supposedly based on one that exists in Chicago. But city officials there told the Daily Oklahoman their ordinance "does not prohibit banners promoting religious or social advocacy organizations and their messages."

Second, the ordinance was passed, apparently, without full investigation by our city staff. When asked whether the Chicago ordinance had been tested in the courts, Oklahoma City's attorney, William West, responded that his office couldn't determine that. Nor did the council discuss whether the ordinance violated constitutional law.

Several citizens at Tuesday's council meeting raised the issue, and several law professors and private attorneys have as well. But the possibility of a legal challenge doesn't seem to bother enough council members to have at least deferred the vote. And a legal challenge they may have — costing taxpayers money to defend the unnecessary and cloudy policy.

Third, as one citizen said during the meeting, if the banners had quoted the Rev. Martin Luther King, Jr., saying "Keep hope alive," no one would have objected. It's pretty clear somebody at City Hall doesn't want homosexuals saying who they are, publicly.

Now, even Rev. King's message might not be allowed. Now, the city manager gets to decide what's "social advocacy" and what's not, what's a religious message and what's not. Does he also get to decide who gets a permit to gather for a rally in a park promoting a candidate for office or carry signs that object to tax increases or promote a message of evangelism or world peace?

It remains to be seen what, if anything, a legal challenge to this policy will bring, beyond a lot of attorney's fees. I just wish the council had thought about that first — to say nothing of thinking about ways to open the city to diversity rather than closing it.

E p i l o g u e

As predicted, Cimarron Alliance filed a lawsuit in federal court, and in September 2002, U.S. District Judge Robin J. Cauthron ruled the restrictive ordinance and the earlier removal of the banners an unconstitutional infringement on Cimarron's right to free speech. It was back to the drawing board for the city.

By this time, the city manager's office wanted out of the dispute and tried to pass the hot potato on to Oklahoma Gas & Electric — the public utility responsible for the light poles — but OG&E said no thanks.

So in 2003, the Council adopted a policy that prohibits only commercial messages (e.g. private businesses) or obscenities from banners or bus stops, and I'm told by the city attorney's office, those are the only screens used for banner acceptance today. So game over, but not without damage done.

Oklahoma City still struggles with its attitude toward its gay citizens as many non-urban, mid-American cities do — particularly those communities strongly influenced by churches and religious groups that believe homosexuality is a sin.

With the new policy in place, Cimarron applied to the city to hang banners for its 2006 gay pride parade, and up they went, no muss no fuss.

The gay and lesbian community has strengthened its positive influence here, in no small part because it stood up for its legal rights in this banner brouhaha. The Cimarron Alliance has grown in size and stature and works against discrimination particularly in job security, adoption and bullying. There is also a separate, growing political action committee that actively – and generously – supports or opposes candidates for office.

Gay-owned businesses have multiplied and "come out" in Oklahoma City, as well. In 2005, Monty Milburn, a realtor who formed a community-wide network of businesses owned or run by gays or lesbians or those that simply want to engage in commerce with the gay community, launched the Diversity Business Association. As of September 2007, DBA listed more than 200 members in its directory.

Humphreys clearly bought more trouble for himself and the city by overreacting to banners on light poles, but the gay community seems to have gotten a boost from it, crazy as that may seem.

I remember what Mike Easterling, then editor of the weekly Oklahoma Gazette, said to me when we talked about the controversy.

"Even though Humphreys is the mayor of a deeply conservative city, on a daily basis he deals with visitors and business and political leaders from other cities – places where members of the gay and lesbian community long have played a full and active role in civic life. They must find it a little odd – if not downright goofy – for a mayor to take to the pages of his local daily newspaper and damn an entire segment of his city's population, especially over such a benign issue as street banners.

"Humphreys is going to think what he wants to think about homosexuals, but he needs to understand that his hostility toward that community is not shared by people in other parts of the country or world, or even by many people here," Easterling said.

❦

NO WELCOME MAT HERE
November 2006

"This measure adds a new section of law to the [state] constitution ... It defines marriage to be between one man and one woman. It prohibits giving the benefits of marriage to people who are not married. It provides that same-sex marriages in other states are not valid in this state. It makes issuing a marriage license in violation of this section a misdemeanor."

here are nine state questions on the November election ballot, most having to do with economic development, taxation and education.

One question, SQ 711, see above, stands out among them all. First, because it's the shortest; second, because it's unfair; and third, because it's likely to end up in court. In a frenzy to protect our homes, marriages, wives, husbands and children from the threat of homosexuality, our state legislators watched Massachusetts grant marriage licenses to individuals of the same sex and panicked.

Now we, the voters, must decide whether to change the state constitution to say who can be married and who cannot; who has the right to live in union, adopt children, visit loved ones in hospitals, pick up children at school, derive spousal health care and other benefits, and who does not.

If you believe polls, nearly 60 percent of voters support this ban — not as many as last week, but still enough to pass it. In a world gone haywire, I suppose people desperately want to believe in the "sanctity" of at least one thing. So they've lighted on marriage and want to prohibit gays from messing it up for the rest of us. As if marriage isn't already messed up with 50 percent ending in divorce. But that's another story.

Passage of this amendment is the same thing as saying to gay people, straight people, business people and others who want to live in a tolerant place that encourages a lively mix of people, "You're not welcome here." Or rather saying, "You can come on and live here with the rest of us but not LIKE the rest of us." It's not a good way to advertise a warm, open city, and it's sure not consistent with business' goal to invite a creative class, including gay people, into our state.

Regardless of how one feels about marriage or homosexuality, this amendment is an act of intolerance. Oklahoma law already bans gay people from the rights and responsibilities of civil marriage and already prohibits gay people from adopting children. This puts an exclamation point on that sentiment.

Who knows what the passage of this amendment might mean legally? Several constitutional lawyers believe it even means heterosexual people living in common-law marriages and civil unions could be denied the benefits of marriage. Some believe it will so alarm employers that they may deny benefits to employees even if they just suspect they are in same-sex relationships.

If the initiative passes, it will guarantee one thing: a lot of (expensive) lawsuits challenging the federal constitutionality of this provision on the grounds that both equal protection and due process are being denied. They might win.

Oklahomans may not be comfortable with homosexuality, but we are known to be fair-minded people. Hopefully, voters will come to see the basic injustice in this shortsighted and unfair ban that speaks not to our proud, welcoming hospitality, but instead, shuts the door on friends and neighbors who could enrich our communities, our businesses and our lives.

Epilogue

I was wrong about Oklahomans and their support of a ban on gay marriage. An amendment to the state's constitution was approved in November 2006, by nearly 75 percent of those who voted. I was wrong, too, that a legal challenge would come on the heels of the vote, though some are being considered. Nor is Oklahoma alone in this: Only Massachusetts allows gays to marry, and 26 states amended their constitution to ban them. A few states allow civil unions or specific rights for gay couples.

In spite of this resounding sentiment against giving gay people the right to marry, there has been political progress for gays here. Jim Roth, an attorney and former deputy to a long-time Oklahoma County Commissioner, was elected countywide to serve as one of three commissioners in 2002 and was re-elected in 2006. An openly gay man, Roth did not campaign about gay rights, but rather on his experience and knowledge of the office and the responsibilities of managing Oklahoma County affairs.

In May 2007, Gov. Brad Henry appointed Roth to fill the unexpired term of a resigning state Corporation Commissioner, one of three statewide officials with the responsibility of regulating much of the activity in the oil, gas, electrical and communications industries in the state. Roth will run for election to finish out this term in 2008 and if elected, must run again for a full six-year term in 2010. He is the first openly gay statewide official in Oklahoma with support in the gay, straight, conservative, liberal, Republican and Democrat ranks.

Also in 2006, Al McAffrey, a Democrat businessman, former police officer and AIDS activist from Oklahoma City's downtown district, ran as an openly gay candidate for the state Legislature and won.

As for my position on gay marriage, it's best stated on buttons and bumper stickers seen around Oklahoma during the marriage amendment vote: "Let gays marry. Let them suffer like the rest of us."

EIGHT

WHAT MATTERS MOST

A PASSOVER PRIMER
APRIL 1995

 e're beginning to get ready for Passover at our house, the Jewish holiday celebrating the ancient Hebrews' freedom from slavery in Egypt.

This is the historical basis for the holiday, but for me, Passover is actually a celebration of the matzo ball, and thank God for that, because what's a holiday without *schmaltz*[1]?

But now you ask: Aren't all holidays filled with plenty of schmaltzy, warm emotion? Yes, *shmendrick*[2], but at Passover, the schmaltz (two tablespoons, melted) is mixed in with six eggs separated, a cup of matzo meal bought, some salt and pepper and after a little of this and a little of that, you have matzo balls.

Schmaltz is a Yiddish[3] word for chicken fat which can't be avoided at Passover, and who wants to anyway. Jews have a tendency to run high cholesterol, which, considering schmaltz, chopped liver, cheese blintzes[4] and *kugel*[5], is easy to figure.

The story of Passover is the story of a great struggle for freedom. For years, the Jews in Egypt had been doing lots of heavy lifting for one of the big Pharaohs who was a miserable excuse for a leader and the first in a long line of tyrants. That was followed, finally, by an exodus and 40 nightmarish years of wandering through the desert with not much more

[1] Rendered chicken fat (Grandma says to make it really tasty, render it in a good pot with some onion.)

[2] A dunce; someone for whom no one has any use; a term without gender but rarely applied to a woman

[3] A language derived from a combination of Hebrew and German and my mother-in-law's first language spoken in her home in Enid, Okla.

[4] Russian pancakes stuffed with cheese, fruit or better yet, both

[5] A delicious noodle pudding

to eat than matzo (unleavened bread), which looks like road-kill Wonder Bread left out in the sun to dry and doesn't taste much better than it looks unless you spread lots of butter on it, which brings us back to the cholesterol problem.

There are many important things about Passover, but for me, none so important as food. For each significant event that befell us in The Days of Old, there is a delicious dish to symbolize it, eaten with much explanation and fanfare at Seder, the Passover dinner and service. Besides, what's a celebration without racking up a few more triglycerides? Gluttony is my point.

Jewish tradition actually speaks to gluttony at Passover. Because slouching was prohibited in Egyptian bondage, the Seder is to be enjoyed from a reclining position.

Personally, I interpret this thusly: After four helpings of chopped liver and six leaden matzo balls in chicken soup, reclining is all you can manage. I also recommend wearing a trench coat or tent, so you can fill up without having to loosen your pants or skirt in the middle of the meal, which is endless with lots of praying and arguing *in mitn derinnen*[-6].

In fact, I have never attended a Seder when an argument didn't break out over whether Jews in America are too much assimilated, whether Uncle Moishe was really a socialist or just grumpy, whether we should be sending more or less aid to Israel, whether most hotel bathtubs are clean enough for bathing or that age-old debate: Whether the best matzo balls should be light and fluffy or hard enough to lob into enemy territory.

My favorite dish among the traditional ones is *charoses*, a mix of chopped apples and pecans, cinnamon and Passover wine. Yes, from the great vintners Mogen David and Mr. Manischewitz come two of the worst wines ever squeezed out of the *nebuchal*[-7] grape, but either is plenty good enough for cooking.

Charoses is served as a symbol of the mortar and bricks the Jews were

---

[-6] Loosely translated, "in the middle of everything, this too?"

[-7] Pathetic. Actually, worse than pathetic.

forced to make for those *fahrshtunkinah*⁻⁸ Pharaohs and their pyramids. The work was hard in those days, but eating charoses with homemade horseradish spread on a piece of matzoh is a *machiah*⁻⁹. If you want to try it, or the almighty matzo ball, call me for the recipes, but don't expect much in the way of exact measurements. As Sara Kasdan wrote in a cooking classic, "If one spoonful is good, so two is better!"

If you only have time for a shortened version of the Passover Seder, my friend told me recently about a prayer that works for all Jewish holidays.

"They tried to kill us. We won. Let's eat."

Whether your choice is matzo balls at Seder or a honey-baked ham for Easter Sunday brunch, I say *L'chaim*⁻¹⁰ to you.

And may you know peace, freedom, a few words of Yiddish and a case of indigestion worth every bite.

⁻⁸ Bad, smelly, rotten, rotten, rotten
⁻⁹ A true pleasure
⁻¹⁰ To life!

MILLENNIUM MADNESS

JANUARY 2000

or nearly one year, my family planned our millennium celebration. No airplanes, no airports, no dependence on air traffic controllers. No huge crowds. No risky hub cities. No computer-run subways or mass transit systems.

No exorbitant hotels or crowded restaurants. No muss, no fuss. Just a pleasant drive west to our favorite getaway in New Mexico and an at-home celebration with family and closest friends.

Ah, friends. Ah, family.

You can't live without 'em and you can't kill 'em.

Ultimately, we pulled it off — 14 people and two dogs, huge dogs, spilling out of one small, rustic mountain house and a borrowed apartment. Well, eventually two borrowed apartments, having something to do with too much closeness, too little comfort.

And it was monumental; madly and millennially monumental. We had lots of home cooking, lots of blazing fires, lots of music, games, hikes, excursions, newcenturyspeak and oldcentury reminiscences. Martha (Stewart, of course) would have been proud. We used lots of Her recipes and talked a lot — doesn't everyone in this century? — about Her new IPO.

Our ages ranged from 7 to 84, with several stops for adolescence, post-adolescence and menopause in between. But, above all, it was kin and kissin' kin, and after 10 days I'll put our challenges up against any Y2K emergency grid center anywhere.

We had two cases of the flu, sequentially, complete with emergency room visits and meals on wheels; a long, steep driveway made impassable by snow, but only one unplanned fire in the kitchen. We lost car keys, a lot of money to a locksmith, a cart of groceries, a shuttle bus, cell phones, jackets and an airplane ticket.

Alternately, and in descending numbers of years, we lost our patience with crowdedness, clutter, wet towels on the couch, dogs in sleeping bags, clogged toilets, ski slope lift lines, restaurants slow to handle 10 or more of us at one sitting, rowdy grandchildren, kids on the phone, kids online, kids spread out everywhere.

Early on New Year's Eve, we visited the home of other friends and their family. They had a beautiful cocktail party in a clean house with well-dressed and smiling children. Oh God.

After that failure-by-comparison, we went home, and I lost it over dirty laundry on the dining room table and how long it took to carve the damn roast. My husband grumped over the treasured and long-saved bottles of Lafitte-Rothschild wine now turned to fine French vinegar. Grandpa lost it over rude and disorganized grandchildren; sisters out-bossed each other in the kitchen; friends out-shopped each other. Nobody knew who was going where or in which car or by what time. Tempers flared, teeth gritted.

Y2K bugs? Hell, this crowd's been buggin' each other for years and have passed some of these same bugs along to family and friends all our lives. Some we've worked out, some we haven't. But above all else, we were here, for and with one another, and I wouldn't have been anywhere else.

We tossed crappy Mylar confetti high in the air, popped corks, drank champagne out of even crappier plastic flutes, and watched a bunch of joyous revelers in Times Square, all of us squeezed around a borrowed seven-inch television screen. Then half of us went to bed and didn't mind a bit, and the other half did whatever you do after midnight when you're so carefree that nothing bugs you.

Our vacation wasn't perfect, but neither are we, my family and my friends.

Happily, most people seemed to have passed the millennium mark much the way we did — with a lot of anticipation and chaos mixed with laughter, muss and fuss, after all. Yes, there was a little grousing and a few snafus, but no bugs so big or momentous as to disrupt the most common, central and cohesive bond in all of our lives, our family and our friends.

Corny it is, but as it turns out, we are one for all, and all for one. And here's to all of us.

UNVEILING THE POSSIBLE
MAY 1991

few days after my mother died, a wise friend said eventually this would all become part of my history. I could not believe that.

Nearly all day every day for months, I felt that an essential part of me had been torn away, that I was badly broken, not at all whole, and was standing, if at all, on either side of a trembling, quake-like crevice. This feeling was so pervasive, I couldn't imagine it ever giving way to acceptance of her absence and my loss. This is it, I thought. I have lost my mother, my source, my center, myself.

My friend guessed this acceptance would begin to happen around the time of the unveiling of my mother's grave stone, a Jewish ritual held more or less one year after a death. This custom derives pragmatically, as do many things in Judaism, from ancient practices. Jews once buried their dead in open fields, moved on in their nomadic culture, waited a year for the natural process of decomposition, then returned and removed the bones, burying them finally in ossuaries or underground caves.

Throughout those months, the official period of mourning went on, but not until the final burial in the ossuary did the mourning end and the permanent markings were made in stone at the burial site. Today we modify this custom and, after a conventional funeral, wait a year to unveil and erect a gravestone.

For me, the year has been in some ways a gift, in some ways a necessity and in another way, a kind of command. I expected sadness and sorrow, but I also unrealistically expected that I, a modern and in-control-of-my-emotions kind of woman, would grieve and then finish grieving. I did not, and I have not.

I needed the year and will need more. I'm grateful there has been this time of allowed, almost prescribed grieving. My misery has not only been sanctioned, it has been expected.

It is 20th century folly to tell yourself that your mother is gone, but since everyone loses someone they love, you can get over this. The ragged emptiness may give way to a milder, more easily mended pain, but this is not something you get over.

Still, this unveiling is also a command for me to get on with the business of living my life. It is not possible to do that, I think, if you have not had time to feel death.

For the last year, it has been my mother's illness and death that has haunted and surrounded me and almost become my own story.

Now as we lay a stone beside her grave, marking both the spot of her burial and the end of one phase of mourning, I feel I am unveiling, finally, the possibility of making her rich, full life, and not just the pain of her death, part of her story and my history.

WHAT MATTERS MOST
MAY 1999

hroughout the evening of May 3, 1999, when the now-infamous F-5-rated, quarter-mile wide, powerful, deadly tornado struck Oklahoma City, my daughter and I watched television weather reporters very carefully. The precise locations of intersections predicting where the twister was headed next and its exact arrival times at those streets, were flashed on the screen accompanied by the increasingly tense voices of meteorologists. As we began to recognize areas on the maps and names of familiar nearby neighborhoods, the announcer warned all of us in Oklahoma County to seek shelter.

OK, we said, looking at each other with a little fear and a lot of determination. Seek shelter we will.

We live in a close-in downtown neighborhood, built in the Twenties, and most of the houses, including our own, have basements. Yes, we were jittery, but I reassured her. After all, that's a parent's job, isn't it? Reassure them even when you haven't a clue if what you're saying is true.

"What matters," I said, "is that we are safe and together."

"And we will be safe in the basement, so let's get going."

Down we went, hauling flashlights and batteries, a few candles and some matches, a couple bottles of water, a portable phone, portable television (more batteries), some blankets and pillows, homework (her priority, not mine, but, hey, I was impressed) and of course, the dog.

After setting up shop, I remembered all my stuff. Like a high-tech scanner, my mind ran a fast inventory over the house — my things, my husband's things, the kids' things. Things everywhere. Years and years worth of things brought back from special travels. Things from birthdays, knick knacks, dresses, baubles and beads.

Should I worry about the computers or cars or VCR or my husband's new stereo? Nope, not now.

Clothes, jewelry or the great shoes I just bought on sale? The hell with them. How about the furniture, rugs, china? Nope. Don't care.

Oh, gosh. Paintings and books and Grandma's keepsakes. Nice, if there were time, but there's not.

I looked around me in the basement, and suddenly none of that mattered much. If all of it were all blown off the face of the earth this very night, would it really matter?

For a lot of people, everything they owned was blown off the face of the earth that night. I hope they survived with the people they cared about, and, sadly, 44 people in our city did not.

Everything that mattered to me was right there with me. Everything else was replaceable. Not easily, not cheaply, not without dislocation and loss. But really, none of it counts. I told myself, I have my family, my trusty dog and my memories ...

"Photos!" I said to my daughter, with a new sense of urgency. "I want the pictures!"

"And my journals," she said to me. Her growing-up life, day by day, since she was a young girl.

So back up we went, dashing frantically through the house, grabbing photo albums, pictures in frames, pictures off walls, diaries, travel journals, baby books — everything that helped us remember how and where we'd lived, how we'd looked and who had been there with us.

No matter how much we shop and spend and collect and stash and store, memory is all we own. And post-50, I've noticed I don't own as much of that as I used to, so photos and chronicles are a must.

As we watched the growing storm, fearful for those to the south and east of us, we were lucky. Piled up together in the basement looking at years of memories — "God, Mom, how could you have worn your hair like that!" and "Yes, you definitely were a goofy looking baby" — we had all we needed.

Dishes break. Furniture wears. Cars rust. Computers become obsolete. Shoes stink. Clothes get too tight. Jewelry fades. Flowers die. Hours fly. Things pass by. They can all be blown away. But love stays.